Dillard's Presents

Southern Living
Christmas
COOKBOOK
Cooking · Entertaining · Giving

benefiting Ronald McDonald House Charities

Dillard's Presents

Southern Living
Christmas
COOKBOOK
Cooking · Entertaining · Giving

RONALD MCDONALD
HOUSE CHARITIES

benefiting Ronald McDonald House Charities

Merry Christmas

from all your friends at Dillard's.

We are proud to support the
Ronald McDonald House.

_____

The purchase of this book helps families of seriously ill children have a comfortable haven near their child.

Thank you for your generosity.
May your family have a wonderful holiday season
and a healthy and prosperous 2017.

_____

CONTENTS

HOLIDAY STYLE

From doors and mantels to trees and tabletops, we offer inspiration for bringing merriment to every room.

Cozy up!
The holidays can be hectic. Take a break to enjoy the warmth of your decorated home.

WELCOME HOME!

Nothing says welcome like a personal touch at the front door!

① Welcome your guests inside with a cheerful holiday wreath. Add fresh red and white berries for a natural touch. **②** Create small vignettes with keepsakes such as these holiday chapels. Mixing in fresh or dried greenery not only fills space but also adds the scent of the holiday season. **③** Decorate a vintage piece. Take an old sleigh and liven it up with a mix of ribbon and rustic ornaments. **④** Embellish the outdoors. Flank the entryway with electric-lit presents for an overall warm glow. Items featured are available at Dillard's and Dillards.com.

TRIM THE TREE

Adorn the tree with vintage ornaments and colorful embellishments for a dazzling update on the traditional tree.

1 Finish off the tree with an elegant topper adorned with burlap-striped ribbon for a strong focal point. **2** Disperse signature ornaments throughout the tree to add character. Have an eclectic mix of old and new ornaments to bring sentiment and new memories to your yearly traditions. **3** Celebrate the season with ornament sets perfect for any festive tree. **4** Jazz up the banister and add fresh garland and oversize ornaments to complete the look.

Deck the halls

Too much color on the tree? Don't worry about having too much color—simplify by adding gold and silver ornaments to balance out all of the bright color.

DRESS UP THE MANTEL

The mantel is the easiest place to add instant holiday cheer.

❶ Dress up your bar with holiday decorations. Switch out the traditional bar cart with old wine barrels placed in convenient spots throughout the room. ❷ Add gifts and smaller decor to the fireplace hearth to complete the festive mood. Simple touches go a long way in the big picture! ❸ Fresh berries and garland make the perfect addition to any candle votive. Always keep lit candles in glass containers, away from the greenery.

SET FOR
THE SEASON

*Bring in festive elements to set the table, such as garland
and holiday figurines to top off the overall look.*

1 Up your garland game by adding ribbon and a strand of lights. **2** Instead of monogramming the stockings, give each family member a different stocking hanger. **3** Don't be afraid to mix and match this holiday season. Use whites, solids, and patterns for your table place settings. **4** Embellish your space with a simple glass garland to jazz up the tree, mantel, or holiday table!

Be our guest

Create a festive table
that is big on impact yet
simple to execute.

TREE ALL AGLOW

Gather around a beautiful Christmas tree.

❶ Play with shapes when using similar-toned ornaments. This gives the tree a polished, dynamic look.
❷ Ornaments don't belong just on the tree. Place them with other holiday pieces on the buffet, side tables, or down the center of your dinner table. ❸ Simplify the dinner table by adding touches of gold and silver for a warm, neutral glow.

CREATE A FESTIVE ENTRYWAY

Add inspiration to your holiday doorway with festive accent pieces.

1 Nothing states "welcome home" like the simple touch of a holiday wreath. **2** Bring the holiday decor to the porch and enjoy the season outside. **3** Artwork doesn't have to hide inside. Display your seasonal art in a covered outdoor space for a welcoming touch.

Cinnamon Roll Waffles with Bananas Foster Sauce, page 34

Spiced Praline Apple Cake, page 27

Cheesy Sausage-and-Croissant Casserole, page 30

Chicken-and-Cheese Mini Waffle Sandwiches, page 41

BREAKFAST GOODIES

Wake up Christmas morning to heavenly aromas
fresh from the oven. No alarm clock needed.

CHRISTMAS MORNING CINNAMON ROLLS

Make sure your butter is very soft when you spread it on the rolled dough so the dough doesn't tear.

MAKES 16 rolls • **HANDS-ON:** 30 minutes • **TOTAL:** 3 hours, 40 minutes, including icing

CINNAMON ROLLS:
Vegetable cooking spray
1   (¼-ounce) envelope active
    dry yeast
¼   cup warm water (105° to 115°F)
1   cup plus 1 teaspoon
    granulated sugar
4   ounces (½ cup) butter,
    softened
1   teaspoon table salt
2   large eggs, lightly beaten

1   cup milk
1   tablespoon fresh lemon juice
5   cups bread flour
¼   teaspoon ground nutmeg
4   ounces (½ cup) very
    soft butter
½   cup firmly packed light
    brown sugar
1   tablespoon ground
    cinnamon
1   cup toasted chopped pecans

CREAM CHEESE ICING:
1   (3-ounce) package cream
    cheese, softened
2   tablespoons butter, softened
2¼ cups powdered sugar
1   teaspoon vanilla extract
1 to 2 tablespoons milk

1. Make the cinnamon rolls: Lightly grease (with cooking spray) 2 (9-inch) square pans. Stir together the first 2 ingredients and 1 teaspoon of the granulated sugar in a glass measuring cup; let stand 5 minutes.

2. Beat ½ cup softened butter at medium speed with a heavy-duty electric stand mixer until creamy. Gradually add ½ cup of the granulated sugar and 1 teaspoon salt, beating at medium speed until light and fluffy. Add the eggs and next 2 ingredients, beating until blended. Stir in the yeast mixture.

3. Stir together 4½ cups of the flour and nutmeg. Gradually add the flour mixture to butter mixture, beating at low speed 1 minute or until well blended.

4. Heavily flour a flat surface; turn dough out, and knead until smooth and elastic (about 5 minutes), adding up to ½ cup more of the flour as needed to prevent dough from sticking. Place the dough in a lightly greased (with cooking spray) large bowl, turning to grease top. Cover and let rise in a warm place (80° to 85°F), free from drafts, 1½ to 2 hours or until doubled in bulk.

5. Punch dough down; turn out onto a lightly floured surface. Roll into a 16- x 12-inch rectangle. Spread with ½ cup very soft butter, leaving a 1-inch border around edges. Stir together the brown sugar, cinnamon, and remaining ½ cup granulated sugar, and sprinkle sugar mixture over butter. Top with the pecans.

6. Roll up the dough, jelly-roll fashion, starting at 1 long side; cut into 16 slices (about 1 inch thick). Place the rolls, cut sides down, in prepared pans. Cover with plastic wrap.

7. Let the rolls rise in a warm place (80° to 85°F), free from drafts, 1 hour or until doubled in bulk.

8. Make the icing: Beat the cream cheese and 2 tablespoons butter at medium speed with an electric mixer 3 to 4 minutes or until creamy. Gradually add the powdered sugar, beating at low speed until blended. Stir in the vanilla and 1 tablespoon of the milk. Stir in up to 1 tablespoon more milk, 1 teaspoon at a time, until smooth.

9. Preheat the oven to 350°F. Bake rolls at 350°F for 20 to 22 minutes or until the rolls are golden brown. Cool in pans 5 minutes. Spread the icing over the rolls. Serve warm.

NOTE: To make ahead, prepare recipe through Step 6, and cover with aluminum foil. Freeze up to 1 month. Thaw covered rolls in refrigerator overnight. Let rise as directed, allowing extra rising time. Bake and ice as directed.

CREAM CHEESE PASTRIES

To make ahead, prepare recipe as directed through Step 5. Refrigerate up to 24 hours.
Let rise as directed in Step 6, allowing a little extra rising time. Proceed as directed in Step 7.

MAKES 4 loaves • **HANDS-ON:** 1 hour • **TOTAL:** 10 hours, 40 minutes, including filling and glaze

CREAM CHEESE PASTRIES:
Parchment paper
1   (8-ounce) container
    sour cream
4   ounces (½ cup) butter, cubed
1   teaspoon table salt
½   cup plus 1 teaspoon
    granulated sugar
2   (¼-ounce) envelopes active
    dry yeast

½   cup warm water
    (100° to 110°F)
2   large eggs, lightly beaten
4   cups bread flour

CREAM CHEESE FILLING:
2   (8-ounce) packages
    cream cheese, softened
¾   cup granulated sugar

1   large egg
2   teaspoons vanilla extract

POWDERED SUGAR GLAZE:
2½ cups sifted powdered sugar
2   teaspoons vanilla extract
3 to 4 tablespoons milk
Garnish: fresh blueberries

1. Make the pastries: Line 2 baking sheets with parchment paper. Heat the first 3 ingredients and ½ cup of the granulated sugar in a small saucepan over medium-low, stirring occasionally, until butter melts. Cool to 100° to 110°F.

2. Combine the yeast, warm water, and remaining 1 teaspoon sugar in a large bowl; let stand 5 minutes. Stir in the sour cream mixture and eggs; gradually add bread flour, beating at low speed with an electric mixer until blended. (Dough will be soft.) Cover and chill 8 to 24 hours.

3. Divide the dough into 4 portions. Turn out each portion onto a heavily floured surface, and knead 4 or 5 times.

4. Make the filling: Beat together the cream cheese, granulated sugar, egg, and vanilla at medium speed with an electric mixer until smooth.

5. Roll each portion of the dough into a 12- x 8-inch rectangle, and spread each rectangle with one-fourth of filling, leaving a 1-inch border. Carefully roll up, starting at 1 long side; press seam, and fold ends under to seal. Place the 4 loaves, seam side down, on prepared baking sheets. Make 6 cuts across each loaf; cover with plastic wrap.

6. Let the loaves rise in a warm place (80° to 85°F), free from drafts, 1 hour or until doubled in bulk.

7. Preheat the oven to 375°F. Bake 2 loaves at a time at 375°F for 15 minutes or until golden brown. (Refrigerate remaining loaves while first batch is baking.)

8. Make the glaze: Stir together the powdered sugar, vanilla, and 3 tablespoons of the milk in a medium bowl. Stir in up to 1 tablespoon more milk, 1 teaspoon at a time, until desired consistency is reached. Drizzle warm loaves with the glaze.

CINNAMON-SUGAR SCONES WITH MASCARPONE CREAM

Traditional high tea often includes scones with clotted or Devonshire cream, available from specialty foods stores. Our recipe uses mascarpone cheese and whipping cream to mimic the thick, creamy, sweet topping that is the perfect accompaniment to a buttery scone.

SERVES 8 · **HANDS-ON:** 16 minutes · **TOTAL:** 1 hour, 6 minutes

Parchment paper
2¼ cups (10.1 ounces) all-purpose flour
⅓ cup granulated sugar
1 teaspoon ground cinnamon
1 tablespoon baking powder

4 ounces (½ cup) cold unsalted butter, cut into small pieces
2½ cups heavy cream
1 large egg, lightly beaten
1 tablespoon water
2 tablespoons turbinado sugar

6 ounces mascarpone cheese
2½ tablespoons granulated sugar
1 teaspoon vanilla extract
¼ teaspoon fresh lemon juice

1. Preheat the oven to 425°F. Line a baking sheet with parchment paper.

2. Whisk together the flour, ⅓ cup granulated sugar, ½ teaspoon of the cinnamon, and baking powder in a large bowl. Cut the butter into the flour mixture with a pastry blender until crumbly and mixture resembles small peas. Add 1 cup of the heavy cream, stirring just until dry ingredients are moistened.

3. Turn the dough out onto a floured surface, and knead about 30 seconds or until smooth. Press or pat the dough into a 7-inch circle.

4. Combine the egg and 1 tablespoon water in a small bowl; brush over the top of the dough. Combine the turbinado sugar and remaining ½ teaspoon cinnamon in a small bowl; sprinkle over the top of the dough. Cut the round into 8 wedges. Place the wedges 2 inches apart on the prepared baking sheet.

5. Bake at 425°F for 18 minutes or until lightly browned. Transfer the scones to a wire rack; cool completely.

6. Combine the mascarpone cheese, next 3 ingredients, and remaining 1½ cups cream in a medium bowl; beat at medium speed with an electric mixer until soft peaks form. Serve the cream with the scones.

ORANGE-GINGER POPPY SEED MINI MUFFINS

*These moist and delicious muffins are a perfect holiday gift from
your kitchen as well as a welcome addition to your holiday brunch.*

MAKES 2 dozen · **HANDS-ON:** 8 minutes · **TOTAL:** 46 minutes

Vegetable cooking spray
1   cup (4.5 ounces)
    all-purpose flour
1½ teaspoons baking powder
¼   teaspoon baking soda
1   tablespoon plus 1 teaspoon
    poppy seeds

¾   cup buttermilk
⅓   cup firmly packed light
    brown sugar
2   ounces (¼ cup) butter,
    melted
2   tablespoons chopped
    crystallized ginger

1   large egg, lightly beaten
2½ teaspoons orange zest
1½ cups powdered sugar
3   tablespoons orange juice

1. Preheat the oven to 400°F. Lightly grease 24 miniature muffin cups with cooking spray. Combine flour, baking powder, baking soda, and 1 tablespoon of the poppy seeds in a bowl; make a well in center of mixture. Combine the buttermilk, next 4 ingredients, and 2 teaspoons of the orange zest; add to dry ingredients, stirring just until moistened.

2. Spoon the batter into the prepared muffin cups, filling two-thirds full.

3. Bake at 400°F for 8 minutes or until lightly browned. Immediately remove from the pans. Cool completely on a wire rack.

4. Stir together the powdered sugar, orange juice, and remaining ½ teaspoon orange zest in a small bowl until smooth. Dip the tops of the muffins into the glaze, and sprinkle with the remaining 1 teaspoon poppy seeds. Let stand 10 minutes or until the glaze is set.

SPICED PRALINE APPLE CAKE

*Ground toasted pecans and chopped apples give this moist, delicately spiced
Bundt cake a comforting appeal. Serve without the rich praline glaze as a snack or coffee cake.*

SERVES 12 • **HANDS-ON:** 28 minutes • **TOTAL:** 4 hours, 6 minutes, including glaze

CAKE:

Shortening

1 cup pecans, toasted and cooled

2½ cups (11.25 ounces) all-purpose flour

2 teaspoons apple pie spice

1 teaspoon baking powder

½ teaspoon baking soda

½ teaspoon table salt

8 ounces (1 cup) butter, softened

2 cups firmly packed light brown sugar

4 large eggs

1 teaspoon vanilla extract

1 (8-ounce) container sour cream

2½ cups finely chopped peeled Fuji apples

PRALINE GLAZE:

½ cup firmly packed light brown sugar

2 ounces (¼ cup) butter

¼ cup half-and-half

1 teaspoon vanilla extract

1 cup powdered sugar

Garnishes: dried apple chips, toasted pecan halves

1. Make the cake: Preheat the oven to 350°F. Grease (with shortening) and flour a 12-cup Bundt pan. Process the pecans in a food processor until finely chopped. Whisk together the pecans, flour, and next 4 ingredients in a bowl.

2. Beat 1 cup butter at medium speed with an electric mixer until creamy. Gradually add 2 cups brown sugar, beating until well blended. Add the eggs, 1 at a time, beating just until blended after each addition. Beat in the vanilla. Add the flour mixture to the butter mixture alternately with sour cream, beginning and ending with flour mixture. Beat the batter at low speed just until blended after each addition. Stir in the chopped apples. Spoon the batter into the prepared pan.

3. Bake at 350°F for 1 hour or until a long wooden pick inserted in the center comes out clean. Cool the cake in the pan on a wire rack 15 minutes; remove from the pan to a wire rack, and cool completely (about 2 hours).

4. Make the glaze: Bring ½ cup brown sugar and next 2 ingredients to a boil in a 2-quart saucepan, whisking constantly; boil 1 minute. Remove from heat; stir in the vanilla. Gradually whisk in the powdered sugar until smooth; stir gently 5 minutes or until the mixture begins to cool and thickens slightly. Spoon immediately over the cooled cake.

Orange-Glazed Monkey Bread

ORANGE-GLAZED MONKEY BREAD

Try this twist on monkey bread for a holiday dessert or breakfast.

SERVES 10 to 12 · **HANDS-ON:** 8 minutes · **TOTAL:** 53 minutes

3 tablespoons butter, softened
½ cup chopped pecans, toasted
2 (16.3-ounce) cans refrigerated jumbo buttermilk biscuits
1 cup granulated sugar

2½ teaspoons firmly packed orange zest
½ cup firmly packed light brown sugar
½ cup (4 ounces) butter, melted

4 ounces cream cheese, softened
½ cup powdered sugar
3 tablespoons fresh orange juice

1. Preheat the oven to 350°F. Grease a 12-cup Bundt pan with 3 tablespoons softened butter. Sprinkle the pecans in the bottom of the prepared Bundt pan.

2. Separate the biscuits, and cut each into quarters. Combine the granulated sugar and 2 teaspoons of the orange zest in a large zip-top plastic freezer bag. Add the biscuit pieces to bag; seal bag, and shake to coat. Arrange the coated biscuit pieces in pan, discarding remaining sugar mixture in bag.

3. Stir together the brown sugar and ½ cup melted butter. Pour over the biscuit pieces.

4. Bake at 350°F for 40 minutes or until top is golden brown. Cool the bread in the pan 5 minutes; invert onto a platter.

5. Place the cream cheese in a medium bowl; beat at medium speed with an electric mixer until creamy. Gradually add the powdered sugar, orange juice, and remaining ½ teaspoon zest, beating at low speed until blended. Drizzle the orange glaze over the warm bread. Serve warm.

BACON AND WHITE PIMIENTO CHEESE TEA SANDWICHES

Spread 8 slices of the bread with pimiento cheese, top with bacon, and serve open-faced, if desired.

SERVES 8 · **HANDS-ON:** 25 minutes · **TOTAL:** 25 minutes

3 tablespoons mayonnaise
1 (3-ounce) package cream cheese, softened
6 ounces sharp white Cheddar cheese, shredded
3 ounces fontina cheese, shredded

3 tablespoons chopped scallions
½ teaspoon Worcestershire sauce
¼ teaspoon ground red pepper
¼ teaspoon table salt

⅛ teaspoon freshly ground black pepper
1 (4-ounce) jar diced pimientos, drained
16 thin white bread slices
6 hickory-smoked bacon slices, cooked and crumbled

1. Place the mayonnaise and cream cheese in a medium bowl; beat at medium speed with an electric mixer until smooth. Stir in the Cheddar cheese and next 6 ingredients. Fold in the pimientos.

2. Cut crusts from the bread slices. Spoon the cheese mixture onto 8 of the bread slices. Sprinkle evenly with the crumbled bacon; top with the remaining 8 bread slices. Cut each sandwich diagonally in half.

CHEESY SAUSAGE-AND-CROISSANT CASSEROLE

This casserole is rich, delicious, and worthy of Christmas breakfast. Gruyère cheese browns beautifully and adds a nutty flavor to the dish. You can sub Swiss cheese if you prefer.

SERVES 8 · **HANDS-ON:** 20 minutes · **TOTAL:** 9 hours, 15 minutes

1 pound hot ground pork sausage (such as Jimmy Dean)
1¼ cups (5 ounces) shredded Parmesan cheese
1 teaspoon table salt

6 scallions, sliced
1 (13.22-ounce) package mini croissants (about 24), torn
Vegetable cooking spray
3 cups milk
1 cup heavy cream

5 large eggs, lightly beaten
2 cups (8 ounces) shredded Gruyère cheese
Garnish: sliced scallions

1. Cook the sausage 8 minutes in a skillet over medium-high heat, stirring to crumble. Toss together the sausage, Parmesan cheese, and the next 3 ingredients; arrange in a 13- x 9-inch baking dish coated with cooking spray.

2. Whisk together the milk and next 2 ingredients; pour over the sausage mixture. Cover and chill for 8 hours.

3. Preheat the oven to 350°F. Uncover the casserole, and sprinkle with the Gruyère. Bake at 350°F for 45 minutes or until golden brown. Let stand 10 minutes.

CRANBERRY STREUSEL MUFFINS

A muffin is always more delicious with a sweet, crumbly topping, and these highlight seasonal cranberries.

MAKES 1 dozen · **HANDS-ON:** 5 minutes · **TOTAL:** 23 minutes

Vegetable cooking spray
¼ cup firmly packed brown sugar
¼ teaspoon ground cinnamon
2¼ cups (10.1 ounces) all-purpose flour
3 tablespoons butter, softened
⅓ cup chopped pecans

⅔ cup granulated sugar
1 teaspoon baking powder
1 teaspoon baking soda
¼ teaspoon table salt
1 cup frozen cranberries, thawed and coarsely chopped
1 cup buttermilk

5⅓ tablespoons (⅓ cup) butter, melted
1 teaspoon vanilla extract
1 large egg

1. Preheat the oven to 400°F. Lightly grease a 12-cup muffin pan with cooking spray. Combine the brown sugar, cinnamon, and ¼ cup of the flour in a small bowl; add the softened butter, rubbing with fingers until crumbly. Stir in the pecans. Cover and chill.

2. Combine the granulated sugar, next 3 ingredients, and remaining 2 cups flour in a large bowl. Stir in the cranberries. Make a well in the center of the mixture. Whisk together the buttermilk and next 3 ingredients; add to the dry mixture, stirring just until moistened.

3. Spoon the batter evenly into the prepared muffin cups, filling three-fourths full. Sprinkle with the streusel mixture, pressing gently to adhere.

4. Bake at 400°F for 18 minutes or until a wooden pick inserted in the center comes out clean. Cool in the pan on a wire rack 5 minutes. Transfer the muffins to a wire rack. Serve warm or cool completely (about 20 minutes).

CINNAMON ROLL WAFFLES WITH BANANAS FOSTER SAUCE

Cinnamon roll waffles are easy to make and have a wonderful chewy texture. Top with decadent bananas Foster sauce for a special Christmas brunch treat. Double the recipe for a crowd.

SERVES 10 · **HANDS-ON:** 20 minutes · **TOTAL:** 20 minutes

2 (17.5-ounce) cans refrigerated jumbo cinnamon rolls
Vegetable cooking spray
1 cup heavy cream
½ teaspoon vanilla extract

4 ounces (½ cup) butter
1 cup firmly packed light brown sugar
⅓ cup dark rum

4 medium-size ripe bananas, sliced
1 cup walnuts or pecans, toasted and chopped

1. Preheat the oven to 200°F. Preheat a Belgian waffle iron to medium. Line a baking sheet with aluminum foil.

2. Separate the cinnamon rolls; reserve icing. Lightly flatten each roll to ½-inch thickness with your fingers. Lightly grease the preheated Belgian waffle iron with cooking spray. Place 1 flattened roll in the center of each cavity of the waffle iron. Cook until golden brown and done. Transfer the waffles to the prepared pan. Keep warm in the oven at 200°F.

3. Beat the cream, vanilla, and icing from 1 can of the cinnamon rolls at high speed with an electric mixer until soft peaks form, reserving the remaining container of frosting for another use. Cover and chill.

4. Melt the butter in a large skillet over medium-high heat; add the brown sugar, and cook, stirring constantly, 2 minutes or until the sugar melts.

5. Remove from heat. Stir in the rum, then carefully ignite the fumes just above the mixture with a long match or long multipurpose lighter. Let the flames die down.

6. Return the skillet to heat. Cook, stirring constantly, 2 minutes or until the sauce is smooth. Add the banana slices; cook 1 minute, turning slices to coat.

7. Top each waffle with about ⅓ cup of the banana sauce and a large dollop of the whipped cream mixture. Sprinkle with the walnuts. Serve immediately.

NOTE: We tested with Pillsbury Grands! Cinnabon Cinnamon Rolls.

BACON-JALAPEÑO BUTTERMILK SCONES

These savory buttermilk scones spiked with bacon and jalapeño peppers make a great accompaniment to breakfast, as well as a tasty midafternoon snack.

SERVES 8 · **HANDS-ON:** 10 minutes · **TOTAL:** 28 minutes

Parchment paper
2 cups (9 ounces) all-purpose flour
2 teaspoons baking powder
½ teaspoon baking soda
½ teaspoon table salt
½ cup cold butter, cut up

⅓ cup pickled sliced jalapeño peppers, drained and minced
2 tablespoons minced fresh chives
8 hickory-smoked bacon slices, cooked and crumbled

3 ounces pepper Jack cheese, shredded
¾ cup buttermilk
1 large egg, lightly beaten
1½ tablespoons buttermilk
¼ teaspoon kosher salt (optional)

1. Preheat the oven to 425°F. Line a baking sheet with parchment paper. Combine the flour and next 3 ingredients in a large bowl. Cut the butter into the flour mixture with a pastry blender or fork until crumbly. Stir in the pickled jalapeño peppers and next 3 ingredients. Whisk together ¾ cup buttermilk and egg. Add to the flour mixture, stirring just until the dry ingredients are moistened and a dough forms.

2. Turn the dough out onto the prepared baking sheet. Shape the dough into an 8-inch circle. Cut the dough into 8 wedges with a floured knife. (Do not separate wedges.)

3. Brush the dough with 1½ tablespoons buttermilk. Sprinkle with the kosher salt, if desired.

4. Bake at 425°F for 16 to 18 minutes or until golden brown and a wooden pick inserted in the center comes out clean. Separate into wedges. Serve immediately or at room temperature.

CHEESY PIMIENTO CORNBREAD

Two iconic Southern staples come together in this savory cornbread.

SERVES 8 to 10 · **HANDS-ON:** 5 minutes · **TOTAL:** 30 minutes

2 ounces (¼ cup) butter

1¼ cups stone-ground yellow cornmeal

¾ cup (3.4 ounces) all-purpose flour

1 teaspoon baking soda

1 teaspoon baking powder

1 teaspoon table salt

¼ teaspoon freshly ground black pepper

4 ounces extra-sharp Cheddar cheese, shredded

1¼ cups buttermilk

2 large eggs

1 (4-ounce) jar diced pimientos, well drained

1. Preheat the oven to 425°F. Place the butter in a 9-inch cast-iron skillet. Place the skillet in oven, and heat at 425°F for 4 minutes or until the butter melts. Remove the skillet from the oven.

2. Meanwhile, combine the cornmeal and next 6 ingredients in a large bowl. Whisk together the buttermilk, eggs, and pimientos; add to the dry ingredients, stirring just until moistened. Pour the batter over the melted butter in the hot skillet.

3. Bake at 425°F for 25 minutes or until golden brown and a wooden pick inserted in the center comes out clean.

Smoky Sausage-and-Grits Casserole

SMOKY SAUSAGE-AND-GRITS CASSEROLE

You can assemble this up to four days ahead and keep in the fridge;
then let it stand at room temp for 30 minutes before baking.

SERVES 12 to 14 • **HANDS-ON:** 30 minutes • **TOTAL:** 1 hour, 25 minutes

Vegetable cooking spray
1½ pounds smoked sausage,
     chopped
½   teaspoon table salt
4½ cups water
1½ cups uncooked
     quick-cooking grits

2   (8-ounce) blocks sharp
     Cheddar cheese, shredded
1   cup milk
1½ teaspoons chopped
     fresh thyme
¼   teaspoon garlic powder

¼   teaspoon ground
     black pepper
4   large eggs, lightly beaten
Garnish: fresh thyme

1. Preheat the oven to 350°F. Lightly grease a 13- x 9-inch baking dish with cooking spray. Brown the sausage in a large skillet over medium-high heat, stirring often, 7 to 9 minutes or until cooked; drain on paper towels.

2. Bring the salt and 4½ cups water to a boil in a large Dutch oven over high heat. Whisk in the grits, and return to a boil. Cover, reduce heat to medium, and simmer 5 minutes or until thickened, whisking occasionally. Remove from heat; add the cheese, stirring until completely melted. Stir in the milk and next 4 ingredients. Stir in the sausage. Spoon the mixture into prepared baking dish.

3. Bake at 350°F for 50 minutes to 1 hour or until golden and cooked through. Let stand 5 minutes before serving.

MINI SAUSAGE AND SPINACH FRITTATAS

Mini frittatas are a grab-and-go Christmas breakfast or brunch. Serve with fruit and toast.

MAKES 1 dozen • **HANDS-ON:** 10 minutes • **TOTAL:** 36 minutes

Vegetable cooking spray
½   pound ground pork sausage
10 large eggs
¼   cup half-and-half
¼   teaspoon table salt

¼   teaspoon freshly ground
     black pepper
⅛   teaspoon ground red pepper
1   cup chopped baby spinach

½   cup chopped drained bottled
     roasted red bell pepper
1½ cups crumbled feta cheese
¼   cup chopped fresh parsley

1. Preheat the oven to 375°F. Lightly grease a 12-cup muffin pan with cooking spray. Brown the sausage in a large skillet over medium-high heat, stirring often, 6 to 8 minutes or until meat crumbles and is no longer pink. Drain.

2. Whisk together the eggs and next 4 ingredients in a large bowl. Layer the cooked sausage, spinach, bell pepper, and 1 cup of the feta cheese evenly in the prepared muffin cups. Pour the egg mixture over the layers.

3. Bake at 375°F for 18 to 20 minutes or until set but not dry. Let stand 5 minutes. Remove frittatas from pan. Sprinkle with the chopped parsley and remaining ½ cup feta cheese before serving.

SAUSAGE-AND-CHEDDAR HOECAKES WITH FRIED EGGS AND TOMATO RELISH

Personalize breakfast with these savory cornmeal cakes topped with eggs the way your guests like them. Finishing them with the fresh and flavorful relish adds texture and color to this hearty holiday offering.

SERVES 6 · **HANDS-ON:** 48 minutes · **TOTAL:** 48 minutes

½ **pound ground pork sausage**
3 **cups boiling water**
2 **tablespoons shortening**
1½ **teaspoons table salt**
2 **cups plain yellow cornmeal**
½ **cup milk**
1 **large egg, beaten**
½ **cup (2 ounces) shredded sharp Cheddar cheese**

¼ **cup olive oil**
2 **cups grape tomatoes, chopped**
¼ **cup finely chopped sweet onion**
2 **tablespoons chopped fresh parsley**
1 **tablespoon chopped fresh garlic**

¼ **teaspoon freshly ground black pepper**
Vegetable cooking spray
6 **large eggs**

1. Preheat the oven to 200°F. Line a baking sheet with aluminum foil.

2. Brown the sausage in a large nonstick skillet over medium-high heat, stirring often, 6 to 8 minutes or until the meat crumbles and is no longer pink; drain. Wipe the skillet with paper towels.

3. Pour 3 cups boiling water over the shortening in a large heatproof bowl, stirring to melt shortening. Stir in 1 teaspoon of the salt and the cornmeal. Stir in the milk. Stir in 1 egg. Fold in the cheese and the sausage.

4. Heat 1 tablespoon of the oil in a nonstick skillet over medium-high. Spoon ¼ cup batter for each of 6 hoecakes into hot oil in the skillet. Cook 3 minutes on each side or until golden brown. Repeat the procedure twice with remaining batter and 2 tablespoons of the oil. Keep the hoecakes warm on the prepared pan in 200°F oven. Wipe the skillet clean after cooking the hoecakes.

5. Combine the tomatoes, next 4 ingredients, ¼ teaspoon of the salt, and remaining 1 tablespoon oil in a bowl.

6. Heat a nonstick skillet over medium. Lightly coat the skillet with cooking spray. Gently break 6 eggs, 3 at a time, into hot skillet; sprinkle evenly with remaining ¼ teaspoon salt. Cook 2 to 3 minutes on each side or until desired degree of doneness.

7. Place 3 hoecakes on each of 6 plates. Top the hoecakes on each plate with 1 egg and ⅓ cup tomato relish. Serve immediately.

CHICKEN-AND-CHEESE MINI WAFFLE SANDWICHES

Pick up chicken strips or nuggets from your grocery store deli or your favorite fast-food restaurant. Frozen, cooked chicken strips will also work.

SERVES 10 · **HANDS-ON:** 15 minutes · **TOTAL:** 15 minutes

1 **(10.9-ounce) package frozen mini waffles**

2 **tablespoons butter, melted**

5 **fast-food fried chicken strips, quartered**

1 **(7-ounce) package cracker-size extra-sharp Cheddar cheese slices**

5 **cooked bacon slices, quartered**

⅔ **cup stone-ground mustard**

⅓ **cup mayonnaise**

¼ **cup maple syrup**

1. Preheat the oven to 400°F. Brush the waffles with butter. Bake the waffles according to package directions.

2. Place the chicken pieces on an ungreased baking sheet. Place 1 cheese square on top of each chicken piece, reserving remaining cheese for another use. Bake at 400°F for 1 to 2 minutes or until cheese melts.

3. Top each of 20 waffles with 1 bacon piece, 1 chicken piece, and 1 waffle. Secure with a wooden pick.

4. Stir together the mustard, mayonnaise, and syrup in a small bowl. Serve with the sandwiches.

NOTE: We tested with Eggo Waffles Minis and Cracker Barrel Extra Sharp Cracker Cuts Cheese.

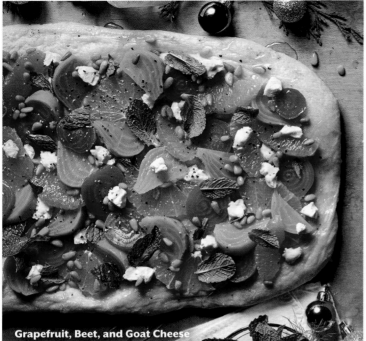

Grapefruit, Beet, and Goat Cheese Flatbread, page 52

Asparagus Parcels and Herbed Lamb Crostini, page 50

Crabmeat Cocktail and Artichoke Canapés, page 57

Ginger-Bourbon Sparkler, page 46

MERRY STARTERS

*Festive cocktails and luxurious nibbles make
five o'clock anywhere a memorable celebration.*

OLD-SCHOOL WHISKEY SOUR

Use your favorite bourbon in this traditional cocktail. Swap the typical maraschino cherry for Luxardo Italian maraschino cherries available online or at specialty foods stores.

SERVES 1 • HANDS-ON: 5 minutes • TOTAL: 5 minutes

¼ cup bourbon
2 tablespoons fresh lemon juice

2 tablespoons Simple Syrup without spices (see opposite)
1 large pasteurized egg white (optional)

½ cup ice cubes
Garnish: maraschino cherry with stem, orange slice

Combine the first 3 ingredients and, if desired, egg white in a cocktail shaker; add ice cubes. Cover with the lid, and shake vigorously until thoroughly chilled and the egg white is foamy (about 30 seconds). Strain into a rocks glass filled with ice.

CLASSIC DIRTY MARTINI

Though the traditional dirty martini uses gin as its base, this "tried-and-true" recipe gives the option for gin or vodka, to suit your preference. An atomizer is a great tool for distributing a thin mist of vermouth in the glass.

SERVES 1 • HANDS-ON: 5 minutes • TOTAL: 5 minutes

½ teaspoon extra dry vermouth
5 tablespoons dry gin or vodka

1 tablespoon Spanish olive juice
½ cup ice cubes

Garnish: large Spanish or other large green olives

Mist a chilled martini glass with the vermouth, or alternatively, add vermouth to a glass and swirl to coat evenly. Combine the gin and olive juice in a cocktail shaker; add ice cubes. Cover with lid, and shake vigorously until thoroughly chilled (about 30 seconds). Strain into the chilled martini glass.

RETRO RUM PUNCH

Serve a blast from the past with this big batch cocktail, perfect for any holiday soiree.

MAKES 9 cups • HANDS-ON: 5 minutes • TOTAL: 5 minutes

1 cup dark rum
1 cup light rum
2 cups pineapple juice

2 cups cranberry juice
2 (12-ounce) bottles ginger beer or ginger ale

Garnishes: frozen cranberries, sliced pineapple

Stir together the dark and light rum, pineapple juice, cranberry juice, and ginger beer in a punch bowl. Add ice. Serve liberally.

SPICED CHOCOLATE STOUT BEER COCKTAIL

Beer cocktails are all the rage this holiday season. Fancy up your favorite chocolate stouts.

SERVES 1 · **HANDS-ON:** 5 minutes · **TOTAL:** 5 minutes

2 **tablespoons brandy**

2 **tablespoons Spicy Simple Syrup (see below)**

1 **(12-ounce) chocolate stout beer**

Combine brandy and Spicy Simple Syrup in a pint glass over ice. Top with chocolate stout, and stir.

NOTE: To make Spicy Simple Syrup, bring 1 cup sugar and 1 cup water to a boil in a saucepan over medium-high. Simmer 5 minutes or until sugar dissolves. Stir in ½ teaspoon each ground red pepper and cinnamon. Cool completely (about 30 minutes). Makes 1 ½ cups

GINGER-BOURBON SPARKLER

This sparkling drink is a great addition to a sumptuous meal. Bitters and ginger act as digestives, and bourbon warms you to your toes. Use a very dry sparkling white wine here.

SERVES 6 · **HANDS-ON:** 6 minutes · **TOTAL:** 1 hour, 11 minutes

½ vanilla bean, split
½ cup firmly packed brown sugar
½ cup chopped fresh ginger

1 cup water
¼ cup fresh lemon juice (2 lemons)
1 cup sparkling dry white wine

¾ cup bourbon
10 dashes of bitters
Garnishes: chopped pineapple, cranberries

1. Scrape the seeds from the vanilla bean pod. Bring the vanilla bean seeds, bean pod, brown sugar, ginger, and 1 cup water to a boil in a medium saucepan; reduce heat, and simmer, uncovered, 10 minutes. Remove from heat; cover and let stand 20 minutes.

2. Pour the ginger syrup through a fine wire-mesh strainer into a bowl; discard solids. Cool completely (about 35 minutes).

3. Stir together the ginger syrup, lemon juice, and next 3 ingredients in a pitcher. Serve over ice in rocks glasses.

RUDOLPH'S TIPSY SPRITZER

When you need a festive holiday cocktail, look no further than this tasty spritzer made with orange juice, lemon-lime soft drink, cherry juice, and vodka. If you want a nonalcoholic beverage, just leave out the vodka and add more orange juice or soft drink.

MAKES 9½ cups • **HANDS-ON:** 10 minutes • **TOTAL:** 10 minutes

5 cups orange juice
2 cups chilled lemon-lime soft drink

1½ cups vodka
½ cup maraschino cherry juice
¼ cup fresh lemon juice

Garnishes: lemon slices, fresh rosemary sprigs

Stir together the first 5 ingredients in a large pitcher; serve over ice.

CAPITAL EGGNOG

No other drink quite epitomizes the holidays like eggnog. Trim the tree and get in the holiday spirit with a cup of this homemade eggnog. Cheers!

MAKES 9 cups • **HANDS-ON:** 35 minutes • **TOTAL:** 4 hours, 5 minutes, including chill time

6 cups milk
2 cups heavy cream
⅛ teaspoon ground nutmeg

12 pasteurized egg yolks
2 cups sugar

Praline or bourbon liqueur (optional)
Freshly grated nutmeg

1. Cook the milk, heavy cream, and ⅛ teaspoon ground nutmeg in a saucepan over medium, stirring occasionally, 5 to 7 minutes or until steaming (about 150°F). Reduce heat to low.
2. Whisk together the egg yolks and sugar in a large saucepan until smooth. Cook over low, whisking constantly, until the mixture reaches at least 160°F (about 25 minutes). Whisk the milk mixture into egg mixture. Cool 30 minutes; transfer to a pitcher. Cover and chill 3 to 24 hours.
3. Pour desired amount of praline or bourbon liqueur into each glass, if desired. Top with the eggnog. Sprinkle with the freshly grated nutmeg.

SPEAKEASY SPARKLER

Our Champagne sparkler gets a lift from moonshine and limoncello. These days you can purchase any number of fine bottles of handcrafted moonshine at your local package store.

SERVES 1 · **HANDS-ON:** 5 minutes · **TOTAL:** 5 minutes

1 sugar cube
Dash of lemon bitters
2½ tablespoons moonshine

2 tablespoons Italian lemon liqueur

⅓ cup Champagne or dry sparkling wine

1. Place the sugar cube in a Champagne flute. Sprinkle the sugar cube with lemon bitters.
2. Combine the moonshine and liqueur in a cocktail shaker; add ice cubes. Cover with lid, and shake vigorously until thoroughly chilled (about 30 seconds). Strain into the prepared Champagne flute, and top with the Champagne.

NOTE: We tested with Midnight Moon moonshine and limoncello for the lemon liqueur.

Speakeasy Sparkler

Smoked Trout Canapés

SMOKED TROUT CANAPÉS

The simplicity of smoked trout on pumpernickel is given a Roaring Twenties-worthy elegance with horseradish-spiked crème fraîche and apple-cucumber relish.

SERVES 15 to 20 • **HANDS-ON:** 29 minutes • **TOTAL:** 1 hour, 44 minutes

½ cup crème fraîche or sour cream
2½ teaspoons prepared horseradish
¾ teaspoon lemon zest
Pinch of kosher salt
34 cocktail-size pumpernickel slices

½ cup finely chopped English cucumber
½ cup finely chopped peeled Granny Smith apple
⅓ cup finely chopped red onion
2 teaspoons fresh lemon juice
1 teaspoon rice vinegar
¼ teaspoon kosher salt

⅛ teaspoon freshly ground black pepper
1 (8-ounce) package smoked trout, skin removed and flaked (about 1¾ cups)
Garnish: fresh watercress leaves

1. Combine the first 4 ingredients in a small bowl. Cover and chill at least 1 hour.

2. Preheat the oven to 350°F. Cut the pumpernickel slices into rounds using a 2-inch round cutter. Place the rounds on a baking sheet. Bake at 350°F for 15 minutes or until lightly toasted, turning once. Cool completely.

3. Combine the cucumber and next 6 ingredients in a bowl. Top each pumpernickel round with a heaping ½ teaspoon of the horseradish cream. Spoon the trout evenly on top of horseradish cream. Top evenly with the apple-cucumber mixture.

MIMOSA GELÉE

These may be made up to a day ahead. Keep tightly covered with plastic wrap, and garnish just before serving.

SERVES 8 • **HANDS-ON:** 8 minutes • **TOTAL:** 3 hours, 8 minutes

1½ cups chilled Champagne or sparkling wine
2 (¼-ounce) envelopes unflavored gelatin

2½ cups orange juice
1 (8-ounce) jar orange blossom honey

Garnishes: orange segments, mint sprigs

1. Pour the Champagne into a large bowl. Sprinkle the gelatin over the Champagne. Set aside.

2. Heat the orange juice and honey in a small saucepan over medium-high 3 minutes or until well blended and thoroughly heated.

3. Add the hot juice mixture to Champagne mixture, and stir 5 minutes or until gelatin dissolves. Pour the mixture evenly into 8 Champagne flutes, and chill 3 hours or until set.

ASPARAGUS PARCELS

Prosciutto-wrapped asparagus in phyllo pastry gets a bright tang from lemon-caper vinaigrette.

SERVES 20 • **HANDS-ON:** 20 minutes • **TOTAL:** 34 minutes

Parchment paper
1½ pounds fresh asparagus (60 thin spears)
2 tablespoons chopped drained capers
1 teaspoon lemon zest

2 tablespoons fresh lemon juice
¼ teaspoon table salt
¼ teaspoon freshly ground black pepper

1 cup olive oil
½ (16-ounce) package frozen phyllo pastry, thawed
10 thin slices prosciutto, halved

1. Preheat the oven to 450°F. Line a large baking sheet with parchment paper. Snap off and discard tough ends of the asparagus. Combine the capers and next 4 ingredients in a bowl. Gradually whisk in ½ cup of the olive oil until blended.

2. Unfold the phyllo on a flat surface. Stack 4 sheets, brushing some of the remaining ½ cup olive oil between sheets. (Keep the remaining phyllo covered with a damp towel.) Cut the stack into 4 squares. (Keep the squares covered with a damp towel.) Repeat procedure to form 20 squares.

3. Working with 1 square at a time, place 1 half slice of the prosciutto on each square. Drizzle each slice with 1 teaspoon lemon-caper vinaigrette. Place 3 asparagus spears on 1 side of each square; roll up, jelly-roll fashion. Place the rolls, seam side down, on prepared baking sheet.

4. Bake at 450°F for 14 minutes or until the phyllo is crisp and golden. Serve immediately with remaining ⅓ cup lemon-caper vinaigrette.

HERBED LAMB CROSTINI

Preserved lemon and harissa-spiked yogurt add Moroccan flair to succulent herbed lamb loin.

SERVES 18 • **HANDS-ON:** 22 minutes • **TOTAL:** 2 hours, 2 minutes

4 cups grape tomatoes
2½ teaspoons kosher salt
1¼ teaspoons freshly ground black pepper
3 tablespoons olive oil
2 tablespoons chopped preserved lemon peel

½ cup plain yogurt
1 tablespoon bottled harissa
1½ tablespoons chopped fresh thyme
1½ tablespoons chopped fresh rosemary
3 garlic cloves, minced

5 lamb tenderloins (1 pound)
36 round baked pita crackers
Garnish: fresh thyme leaves

1. Preheat the oven to 250°F. Arrange the tomatoes in a single layer on a baking sheet. Sprinkle with ½ teaspoon of the salt and ¼ teaspoon of the pepper; toss with 1 tablespoon of the olive oil to coat.

2. Bake at 250°F for 1 hour and 30 minutes or until the tomatoes are softened, turning every 30 minutes. Transfer to a bowl; mash with a fork, leaving some whole. Stir in the preserved lemon peel. Stir together the yogurt and harissa in a small bowl. Cover and chill.

3. Combine herbs and garlic with remaining 2 teaspoons salt and 1 teaspoon pepper in a bowl. Stir in 1 tablespoon of the olive oil. Rub the herb mixture over lamb. Heat remaining olive oil in a large skillet over medium-high. Cook 2 minutes on each side for medium-rare or to desired doneness.

4. Remove from skillet; let stand 5 minutes. Cut the lamb crosswise into ¼-inch-thick slices. Spoon 1 tablespoon tomato mixture onto each cracker. Top with 1 lamb slice and ¾ teaspoon yogurt mixture.

Asparagus Parcels

Herbed Lamb Crostini

GRAPEFRUIT, BEET, AND GOAT CHEESE FLATBREAD

Leave bakery pizza dough at room temperature for 30 minutes for easier kneading.

SERVES 10 · **HANDS-ON:** 20 minutes · **TOTAL:** 2 hours, 5 minutes

- 1½ pounds golden beets
- ⅓ cup water
- 1 pound bakery pizza dough
- Vegetable cooking spray
- ½ tablespoon olive oil
- ¼ teaspoon kosher salt
- ¼ teaspoon freshly ground black pepper
- 6 ounces goat cheese, crumbled
- 2 small grapefruit, peeled and sectioned
- 2 tablespoons fresh mint leaves, thinly sliced
- ¼ cup toasted pine nuts
- 2 tablespoons honey
- ¼ teaspoon coarse sea salt
- Garnish: mint leaves

1. Preheat the oven to 350°F. Trim beet stems to 1 inch; gently wash the beets, and place in a 13- x 9-inch baking dish. Add ⅓ cup water, and cover with aluminum foil.

2. Bake at 350°F for 1 hour or until tender. Uncover and cool completely (about 30 minutes).

3. Meanwhile, remove the pizza dough from refrigerator, and let stand 30 minutes.

4. Increase oven temperature to 425°F. Turn the dough out on a lightly floured surface, and roll into a 17- x 13-inch rectangle (about ¼ inch thick). Place the dough rectangle on a lightly greased (with cooking spray) baking sheet.

5. Brush the dough with olive oil; sprinkle with the kosher salt and pepper. Bake at 425°F for 15 to 20 minutes or until golden brown.

6. Cut the cooled beets into thin slices. Top the crust with beet slices, goat cheese, grapefruit segments, sliced mint, and toasted pine nuts, leaving a ½-inch border. Drizzle the flatbread with honey, and sprinkle with sea salt.

ROASTED FENNEL-AND-PROSCIUTTO FLATBREAD

You can substitute sweet onion for fennel and bacon for prosciutto.

SERVES 10 • **HANDS-ON:** 30 minutes • **TOTAL:** 1 hour, 20 minutes

1   **pound bakery pizza dough**
2   **fennel bulbs**
2½ **tablespoons olive oil**
1   **teaspoon finely chopped fresh thyme**
1   **teaspoon finely chopped fresh oregano**

2   **ounces thinly sliced prosciutto**
Vegetable cooking spray
1½ **cups (6 ounces) shredded fontina cheese**
¼   **teaspoon dried crushed red pepper**

1   **teaspoon coarse sea salt**
1   **tablespoon bottled balsamic glaze**

1. Preheat the oven to 425°F. Line a baking sheet with aluminum foil. Remove the pizza dough from refrigerator, and let stand 30 minutes or until ready to use.

2. Meanwhile, trim and discard root end of the fennel bulbs. Trim the stalks from bulbs, and chop the fronds to equal 2 teaspoons. Thinly slice the fennel bulbs lengthwise, and place on prepared baking sheet. Drizzle with 2 tablespoons of the olive oil. Sprinkle with the thyme and oregano. Bake at 425°F for 35 minutes or until the edges are golden brown.

3. Cook the prosciutto in a large nonstick skillet over medium-high 1 to 2 minutes on each side or until browned and crisp. Break the prosciutto into large pieces.

4. Turn the dough out on a lightly floured surface, and roll into a 17- x 13-inch rectangle (about ¼ inch thick). Place the dough rectangle on a lightly greased (with cooking spray) baking sheet. Brush the dough with remaining 1½ teaspoons olive oil. Bake at 425°F for 15 to 20 minutes or until golden brown. Remove the crust from oven, and increase oven temperature to broil.

5. Top the crust with fontina cheese, fennel slices, and prosciutto. Broil 1 minute. Sprinkle with the dried crushed red pepper, reserved 2 teaspoons chopped fennel fronds, and coarse sea salt. Drizzle with the balsamic glaze.

NOTE: We tested with Acetum Blaze Original Balsamic Glaze.

CHICKEN LIVER MOUSSE CROSTINI WITH PEPPER JELLY

You can also make this mousse in a 1½-quart ovenproof dish instead of small jars if you prefer.

SERVES 12 to 14 · **HANDS-ON:** 35 minutes · **TOTAL:** 2 hours, 35 minutes

4 ounces (½ cup) butter
1 cup finely chopped yellow onion
1 garlic clove, minced
½ cup heavy cream

1 pound chicken livers
½ teaspoon kosher salt
¼ teaspoon freshly ground black pepper

⅔ cup red pepper jelly
1 (8- to 9-ounce) French bread baguette, sliced and toasted

1. Preheat the oven to 300°F. Melt 2 tablespoons of the butter in a small saucepan over medium heat. Stir in the chopped onion. Cover and cook, stirring occasionally, 6 to 7 minutes or until tender. Add the minced garlic, and sauté 10 seconds. Stir in the cream, and bring to a simmer. Cover, reduce heat to low, and cook 6 minutes.

2. Add the remaining 6 tablespoons butter, and cook, stirring constantly, about 1 minute or until the butter is melted and well blended. Remove from heat.

3. Process the chicken livers, kosher salt, black pepper, and onion mixture in a blender or food processor 30 to 45 seconds or until smooth, stopping to scrape down sides as needed.

4. Place 7 (8-ounce) widemouthed ovenproof jars with tight-fitting lids in a 13- x 9-inch baking dish. Divide the liver mixture among jars, filling each halfway. Add warm water to baking dish to a depth of 1¼ inches. Cover jars and baking dish tightly with heavy-duty aluminum foil.

5. Bake at 300°F for 30 minutes or until the mousse is set. Remove from the oven, transfer jars to a wire rack, and cool completely (about 30 minutes). Screw on the lids, and chill 1 hour.

6. Just before serving, spoon 1½ tablespoons red pepper jelly into each jar. Serve with the toasted baguette slices.

NOTE: We tested with Kerr Wide Mouth Half-Pint Jars.

CREAMY SHRIMP DIP
WITH CRISPY WONTON CHIPS

If you don't have time to make fried wontons, use fancy potato chips or crispy tortilla strips.

SERVES 8 to 10 • **HANDS-ON:** 15 minutes • **TOTAL:** 55 minutes, including wonton chips

CREAMY SHRIMP DIP:
- 1 pound large cooked, peeled, and deveined shrimp, chopped
- 2 scallions, finely chopped
- 1 shallot, finely chopped
- ½ cup mayonnaise
- ½ cup sour cream
- 2 tablespoons fresh tarragon leaves, finely chopped
- 2 teaspoons rice vinegar
- ½ teaspoon kosher salt
- ¼ teaspoon freshly ground black pepper

CRISPY WONTON CHIPS:
- Vegetable oil
- 1 (6-ounce) package wonton wrappers
- Kosher salt
- Garnish: sliced fresh chives

1. Make the shrimp dip: Stir together the first 9 ingredients in a medium bowl until well blended. Cover and chill 30 minutes to 1 day.

2. Make the wonton chips: Pour the vegetable oil to a depth of 1 inch into a Dutch oven, and heat over medium-high to 350°F. Cut each wonton wrapper into quarters. Fry, in batches, 15 to 20 seconds on each side or until golden brown and crisp. Drain on a wire rack over paper towels; sprinkle with kosher salt. Serve dip with wonton chips.

Chicken Liver Mousse Crostini with Pepper Jelly

Creamy Shrimp Dip with Crispy Wonton Chips

Crabmeat Cocktail

Artichoke Canapés

CRABMEAT COCKTAIL

Lump crabmeat combines with pineapple, cilantro, lime juice, and avocado for a tropical twist.

SERVES 10 · **HANDS-ON:** 23 minutes · **TOTAL:** 3 hours, 23 minutes, including pickled onion

QUICK PICKLED RED ONION:
- ¾ cup white vinegar
- 3 tablespoons sugar
- ¼ teaspoon table salt
- 1 (8-ounce) red onion, cut into thin half-moon slices and separated
- ½ cup ice cubes

CRABMEAT COCKTAIL:
- 1 pound fresh lump crabmeat, drained
- 1 cup finely chopped fresh pineapple
- Quick Pickled Red Onion
- 5 tablespoons fresh lime juice (about 3 limes)
- 3 tablespoons chopped fresh cilantro

- 1½ tablespoons olive oil
- ½ teaspoon sea salt
- ¼ teaspoon freshly ground black pepper
- 2 jalapeño peppers, seeded and minced
- 1 avocado, coarsely chopped
- Garnish: lime wedges

1. Make the Quick Pickled Red Onion: Bring the vinegar, sugar, and salt to a boil in a nonreactive saucepan over medium-high. Add the onion. Reduce heat to medium-low; cook, uncovered, 1 minute. Remove from heat; transfer to a bowl with the ice cubes. Cover and chill at least 1 hour.
2. Make the Crabmeat Cocktail: Pick the crabmeat, removing any shell. Combine the pineapple and next 7 ingredients in a large bowl; fold in the crabmeat. Cover and chill at least 2 hours.
3. Fold in the avocado to serve. Divide the crab mixture evenly among 10 martini or cocktail glasses.

ARTICHOKE CANAPÉS

Goat cheese and fennel-olive relish give these canapés Mediterranean flair.

SERVES 23 · **HANDS-ON:** 25 minutes · **TOTAL** 1 hour, 20 minutes

- 1 small fennel bulb, sliced
- 1 (14-ounce) can quartered artichoke hearts, drained
- 1 (8.5-ounce) French baguette
- ¼ cup pitted kalamata olives, chopped
- ¼ cup pitted picholine olives, chopped

- 2 tablespoons olive oil
- 2 teaspoons lemon zest
- ⅛ teaspoon red pepper flakes
- 1 (8-ounce) package cream cheese, softened
- 1 (4-ounce) goat cheese log, softened

- 2 teaspoons chopped fresh thyme
- 2 teaspoons fresh lemon juice
- ¼ teaspoon table salt
- Garnish: fresh dill sprigs

1. Preheat the oven to 450°F. Place the fennel in a single layer on 1 side of a rimmed baking sheet; place the artichokes on opposite side. Bake at 450°F for 20 minutes or until the fennel is golden brown, turning once. Transfer the fennel to a cutting board to cool completely (10 minutes). Return the artichokes to oven; bake 10 minutes or until lightly browned. Cool completely (10 minutes).
2. Reduce oven temperature to 350°F. Slice baguette into 46 (¼-inch-thick) round slices; arrange in a single layer on a baking sheet. Bake 10 minutes or until golden. Cool completely (5 minutes).
3. Chop the fennel and combine with the olives and next 3 ingredients in a small bowl.
4. Chop the artichoke hearts. Stir together the cream cheese and next 4 ingredients until smooth. Stir in the artichoke hearts.
5. Spread 2 teaspoons of the cream cheese mixture on each bread slice; top with 1 teaspoon relish.

SMOKED TROUT CROSTINI WITH RADISHES AND DILL CREAM

For an even more colorful spread, replace half the trout with smoked salmon.

SERVES 8 to 10 • **HANDS-ON:** 20 minutes • **TOTAL:** 35 minutes

8   thick, firm white bread slices, crusts removed
1   tablespoon olive oil
½   teaspoon kosher salt
¼   teaspoon ground black pepper

1   (8-ounce) container sour cream
½   teaspoon fresh lemon juice
1   teaspoon prepared horseradish
1   tablespoon chopped fresh dill weed

1¼ cups thinly sliced radishes
1   (8-ounce) smoked trout fillet, flaked into ½-inch pieces
Garnish: fresh dill weed

1. Preheat the oven to 350°F. Cut each bread slice into 4 triangles. Brush with the olive oil, and sprinkle with ¼ teaspoon of the salt and pepper. Place in a single layer on a baking sheet; bake at 350°F for 15 to 20 minutes or until golden.

2. Stir together the sour cream, next 3 ingredients, and remaining ¼ teaspoon salt. Spoon about 1½ teaspoons of the sour cream mixture onto each bread triangle. Top with the radish slices and trout.

TINY TOMATO TARTS

If short on time, substitute frozen phyllo shells for the homemade tarts.

MAKES 24 tartlets • **HANDS-ON:** 30 minutes • **TOTAL:** 50 minutes

½ (14.1-ounce) package refrigerated piecrusts

1 (14.5-ounce) can petite diced tomatoes

1 tablespoon chopped fresh basil

Table salt

Ground black pepper

⅔ cup mayonnaise

½ cup grated Parmesan cheese

¼ cup (1 ounce) freshly shredded Cheddar cheese

¼ cup (1 ounce) freshly shredded mozzarella cheese

Garnish: fresh basil leaves

1. Preheat the oven to 425°F. Unroll the piecrust on a floured surface; roll into a 12-inch circle. Cut into 24 rounds with a 2-inch scalloped round cutter. Press the rounds into bottoms of ungreased miniature muffin cups. (Dough will come slightly up sides.) Prick bottom of dough once with a fork.

2. Bake at 425°F for 5 minutes or until set. Cool in pans 15 minutes. Reduce oven temperature to 350°F.

3. Meanwhile, drain the tomatoes well, pressing between paper towels. Combine the tomatoes and chopped basil in a small bowl; add salt and pepper. Stir together mayonnaise and next 3 ingredients in a medium bowl. Divide the tomato mixture among pastry shells, and top with mayonnaise mixture.

4. Bake at 350°F for 18 to 20 minutes. Serve immediately.

FRIED HOMINY

Dangerously delicious, this is the new popcorn for your next tree trimming party.

SERVES 8 to 10 • **HANDS-ON:** 40 minutes • **TOTAL:** 3 hours, 45 minutes, including spice mix

2 (14.5-ounce) cans white hominy, drained

Canola oil

1 cup (4.5 ounces) all-purpose flour

½ cup plain white cornmeal

¼ cup cornstarch

¾ teaspoon table salt

½ teaspoon ground black pepper

Savory Spice Mix or Cinnamon Spice Mix

SAVORY SPICE MIX:

1 tablespoon chopped fresh thyme

¾ teaspoon table salt

½ teaspoon ground cumin

½ teaspoon ground coriander

½ teaspoon paprika

½ teaspoon ground black pepper

¼ teaspoon ground red pepper

¼ teaspoon dried oregano

CINNAMON SPICE MIX:

¼ cup granulated sugar

¼ cup firmly packed light brown sugar

¾ teaspoon table salt

¼ teaspoon ground cinnamon

⅛ teaspoon ground red pepper

1. Spread the hominy on paper towels in a jelly-roll pan. Chill, uncovered, 3 to 24 hours.

2. Pour 3 inches oil in a Dutch oven. Heat over medium-high to 350°F. Combine the flour and next 4 ingredients; toss, in batches, with hominy. Shake off excess flour.

3. Fry hominy, in batches, 6 minutes or until kernels float to the top; remove and drain.

4. Make the Savory Spice Mix: Combine all ingredients.

5. Make the Cinnamon Spice Mix: Combine all ingredients.

6. Sprinkle hot hominy with desired amount of either Savory Spice Mix or Cinnamon Spice Mix.

SMOKED CHICKEN BUTTERMILK BISCUIT SLIDERS

Tender mini buttermilk chive biscuits are filled with
smoked chicken and creamy pickled okra-studded slaw for a filling appetizer.

SERVES 16 · **HANDS-ON:** 35 minutes · **TOTAL:** 1 hour

Parchment paper
¼ cup sliced red onion
4 ounces (½ cup) cold butter, cut into pieces
2½ cups self-rising soft-wheat flour
2 tablespoons chopped fresh chives
1 cup buttermilk
Self-rising soft-wheat flour
2 tablespoons butter, melted
2½ cups shredded coleslaw mix
½ cup sliced pickled okra
½ cup white barbecue sauce
1 pound smoked chicken, shredded and coarsely chopped

1. Place oven rack in top third of oven. Preheat the oven to 450°F. Line a jelly-roll pan with parchment paper or lightly grease jelly-roll pan. Place the onion in a small bowl; cover with cold water, and set aside.

2. Sprinkle 2 tablespoons of the cold butter over flour in a bowl, and toss. Cut the remaining 6 tablespoons cold butter into the flour with a pastry blender or fork until mixture resembles small peas and dough is crumbly. Cover and chill 10 minutes. Stir in the chives. Add the buttermilk, stirring just until dry ingredients are moistened.

3. Turn the dough out onto a lightly floured surface, and knead 3 or 4 times, gradually adding additional self-rising flour as needed. With floured hands, pat the dough into a ¾-inch-thick rectangle (about 9 x 5 inches); dust the top with flour. Fold the dough over itself in 3 sections, starting with the short end (as if folding a letter-size piece of paper). Repeat 2 more times, beginning with patting the dough into a rectangle.

4. Pat the dough to ½-inch thickness. Cut with a 1¾-inch round cutter, and place biscuits side by side on the prepared jelly-roll pan. (Dough rounds should touch.)

5. Bake at 450°F for 15 minutes or until lightly browned. Remove from oven; brush with 2 tablespoons melted butter.

6. Meanwhile, drain the onion from water. Combine the coleslaw mix, okra, red onion, and white barbecue sauce, tossing to coat.

7. Split the biscuits. Top bottom half of the biscuits evenly with smoked chicken and slaw. Cover with top half of biscuits. Serve immediately.

MARINATED OLIVES AND ALMONDS

A big batch of these antipasti will last in the refrigerator up to a week. It's the perfect snack to serve unexpected holiday company. For extra flavor, use smoked almonds.

SERVES 10 to 12 • **HANDS-ON:** 10 minutes • **TOTAL:** 4 hours, 10 minutes

½ cup extra virgin olive oil
3 garlic cloves, crushed
2 tablespoons grapefruit zest
2 tablespoons fresh grapefruit juice
2 tablespoons red wine vinegar

1 tablespoon chopped fresh thyme leaves
1 tablespoon orange zest
2 teaspoons sugar
1 teaspoon kosher salt

½ teaspoon freshly ground black pepper
4 cups pitted and drained green and black olives
1½ cups roasted salted almonds

1. Stir together the first 10 ingredients in a large bowl. Add the olives; toss with the marinade to coat. Cover and chill 4 to 24 hours.

2. Remove and discard the crushed garlic cloves, and stir in the roasted almonds just before serving. Serve with a slotted spoon.

BENNE-MAPLE ROASTED PECANS

Make these a few days ahead, and chill in an airtight container.

MAKES 4 cups • **HANDS-ON:** 15 minutes • **TOTAL:** 1 hour, 5 minutes

Parchment paper
¼ cup (2 ounces) butter
4 cups pecan halves, toasted
¼ cup firmly packed brown sugar

¼ cup maple syrup
1 tablespoon soy sauce
¾ teaspoon kosher salt
⅛ teaspoon ground red pepper

1 tablespoon sesame oil
2 tablespoons sesame seeds, toasted

1. Line a jelly-roll pan with parchment paper. Melt the butter in a saucepan over medium-high; stir in the pecans and next 5 ingredients. Cook, stirring constantly, 5 minutes or until the syrupy coating on nuts almost evaporates. Stir in the sesame oil; remove from heat.

2. Spread the pecans in the prepared pan; sprinkle with sesame seeds. Cool completely.

INSIDE-OUT HOT BROWN BITES

The signature Kentucky sandwich is reimagined into beautiful bite-size cups.

MAKES 2 dozen • **HANDS-ON:** 45 minutes • **TOTAL:** 45 minutes

Vegetable cooking spray
1½ (5-ounce) containers finely shredded Parmesan cheese
1⅔ cups milk
2 ounces (¼ cup) butter
3 tablespoons all-purpose flour
½ cup (2 ounces) shredded medium Cheddar cheese

⅛ teaspoon kosher salt
⅛ teaspoon freshly ground black pepper
4 ounces thinly sliced deli turkey, cut into 2-inch squares

4 cooked bacon slices, crumbled
½ cup diced fresh tomato
Garnish: fresh flat-leaf parsley leaves

1. Preheat the oven to 350°F. Line 2 baking sheets with aluminum foil, and lightly grease with cooking spray. Lightly grease a 24-cup miniature muffin pan with cooking spray. Spoon the Parmesan cheese by tablespoonfuls ½ inch apart onto each baking sheet, forming 12 (2½-inch) rounds.

2. Bake 1 sheet at 350°F for 7 to 9 minutes or until edges are lightly browned and beginning to set. Working quickly, transfer the cheese rounds to prepared muffin pan, pressing gently into each cup to form shells. Repeat procedure with second baking sheet.

3. Microwave the milk in a microwave-safe measuring cup 30 seconds at HIGH or until warm. Melt the butter in a small saucepan over medium-high. Whisk in the flour; cook, whisking constantly, 1 minute. Gradually whisk in the warm milk. Bring to a boil, and boil, whisking constantly, 1 to 2 minutes or until thickened. Whisk in the shredded Cheddar cheese, kosher salt, and black pepper.

4. Increase the oven temperature to 425°F. Line each Parmesan shell with 2 turkey pieces, and fill each with 1 teaspoon cheese sauce. Bake at 425°F for 5 minutes. Remove from the pan to a wire rack, and top with the crumbled bacon and diced tomato.

SMOKED SALMON JOHNNYCAKES WITH LEMON CRÈME FRAÎCHE

These spicy bites of goodness get a party going. Serve with flutes of Champagne.

SERVES 12 • **HANDS-ON:** 17 minutes • **TOTAL:** 29 minutes

2 cups stone-ground yellow cornmeal

¼ cup (1.1 ounces) all-purpose flour

1¼ teaspoons table salt

¼ teaspoon ground red pepper

1 large egg, lightly beaten

1 cup milk

2 ounces (¼ cup) unsalted butter, melted

1½ tablespoons finely minced jalapeño pepper (½ pepper)

2 tablespoons water

3 tablespoons canola oil

½ cup crème fraîche

1 teaspoon fresh lemon juice

¼ teaspoon freshly ground black pepper

½ pound thinly sliced smoked salmon, cut into 24 equal pieces

12 pickled okra pods, each halved lengthwise

Garnish: lemon zest

1. Combine the first 4 ingredients in a large bowl. Whisk together the egg, next 3 ingredients, and 2 tablespoons water; whisk into flour mixture just until blended.

2. Heat 1 tablespoon of the oil in a large nonstick skillet over medium-high. Drop ½ cup batter, by tablespoonfuls, 1 inch apart, into hot oil. Cook the cakes 1 to 2 minutes on each side or until golden brown. Transfer the cakes to a plate lined with a paper towel. Keep warm. Repeat procedure twice with remaining 2 tablespoons oil and remaining batter.

3. Stir together the crème fraîche, lemon juice, and black pepper in a small bowl until smooth.

4. Place the cakes on a large serving platter. Place 1 salmon piece on the top of each cake. Dollop the cakes evenly with the crème fraîche mixture, and top each with 1 piece of pickled okra. Serve immediately.

PETITE SWEET POTATO BISCUITS WITH PULLED PORK AND SLAW

The sweet potato biscuits freeze beautifully—thaw, bake, and top them just before serving.

MAKES 2 dozen • **HANDS-ON:** 15 minutes • **TOTAL:** 1 hour, 25 minutes, including biscuits

1 cup finely chopped red cabbage
½ cup shredded carrots, chopped
1 teaspoon kosher salt
1 tablespoon mayonnaise
1 tablespoon red wine vinegar
⅓ cup barbecue sauce
¼ cup sliced scallions
Kosher salt

Freshly ground black pepper
12 Sweet Potato Biscuits
2 tablespoons butter, melted
½ pound warm barbecue pork (without sauce), chopped
1 tablespoon chopped fresh chives

SWEET POTATO BISCUITS:
Vegetable cooking spray
1½ cups cooked, mashed sweet potatoes
1 cup buttermilk
6 tablespoons butter, melted
3⅓ cups (13⅓ ounces) self-rising flour
2 tablespoons sugar
⅛ teaspoon baking soda

1. Toss together the first 3 ingredients in a small bowl. Let stand 30 minutes. Rinse and drain well. Whisk together the mayonnaise, vinegar, and 1 tablespoon barbecue sauce in a medium bowl. Stir in the cabbage mixture and scallions. Add salt and pepper to taste.

2. Make the biscuits: Preheat the oven to 400°F. Lightly grease a baking sheet with cooking spray. Stir together the sweet potatoes, buttermilk, and butter in a large bowl. Add 3 cups of the flour, sugar, and baking soda, stirring just until dry ingredients are moistened.

3. Turn dough out onto a lightly floured surface; knead 8 to 10 times, adding up to ⅓ cup more flour to prevent dough from sticking. Roll dough to ¾-inch thickness; cut with a 2-inch round cutter. Place biscuits on the prepared pan. Bake at 400°F for 15 to 20 minutes or until golden brown.

4. Increase oven temperature to 450°F. Split the biscuits, and brush with 2 tablespoons melted butter. Place in a single layer on a baking sheet. Bake at 450°F for 5 minutes or until golden.

5. Top the biscuit halves evenly with pork, remaining barbecue sauce, cabbage mixture, and chives.

WARM BRIE TARTLETS WITH SPICED APRICOT CHUTNEY

Using prepared phyllo shells saves you time when making this sweet-and-savory dish.
Use any leftover chutney as a spread for sandwiches, or spoon over roasted chicken or pork chops.

SERVES 15 • **HANDS-ON:** 33 minutes • **TOTAL:** 33 minutes

2 (1.9-ounce) packages frozen mini-phyllo pastry shells, thawed
½ cup finely chopped onion
1 garlic clove, minced
1 tablespoon olive oil
½ teaspoon ground cinnamon

¼ teaspoon table salt
¼ teaspoon ground cumin
¼ teaspoon ground coriander
1½ cups chopped dried apricots
⅓ cup raisins
¼ cup dried currants

⅔ cup firmly packed light brown sugar
¼ cup apple cider vinegar
½ cup water
1 (8-ounce) Brie round*
Garnish: chopped fresh chives

1. Place the phyllo cups on a serving platter. Sauté the onion and garlic in hot oil in a medium saucepan over medium-high until tender. Stir in the cinnamon and next 3 ingredients; cook 1 minute. Add the apricots, next 4 ingredients, and ½ cup water. Bring to a boil; reduce heat, and simmer 15 minutes or until thickened.

2. Trim and discard the rind from the cheese; cut into 30 (½-inch) pieces. Divide the cheese pieces among the phyllo shells; spoon about 1½ teaspoons of the hot chutney over cheese in each tartlet, reserving remaining chutney for another use. Serve warm.

* Camembert or cambozola cheese may be substituted.

BEEF TENDERLOIN CROSTINI

*Here is a melt-in-your-mouth appetizer that will be the standout of your party
thanks to the ensemble of perfectly seasoned layers and, of course, the grilled tenderloin.*

MAKES 3 dozen · **HANDS-ON:** 45 minutes · **TOTAL:** 1 hour, 35 minutes

CILANTRO SAUCE:
2 teaspoons cumin seeds
1½ cups firmly packed fresh cilantro leaves
⅓ cup olive oil
1 garlic clove
2 tablespoons fresh lime juice
½ teaspoon kosher salt
2 tablespoons water

MANGO-RED ONION RELISH:
½ cup diced red onion
1 teaspoon olive oil
1 large mango, peeled and diced
¼ cup diced red bell pepper
1 jalapeño pepper, seeded and minced
1 tablespoon Champagne vinegar
Table salt
Freshly ground black pepper

BEEF TENDERLOIN:
1 pound beef tenderloin fillets
1 tablespoon olive oil
1 teaspoon kosher salt
½ teaspoon freshly ground black pepper
⅛ teaspoon garlic powder

HERBED CORNBREAD CROSTINI:
2 cups self-rising white cornmeal mix
2 tablespoons sugar
2 large eggs
½ cup sour cream
½ cup buttermilk
4 ounces (½ cup) butter, melted
2 tablespoons chopped fresh chives
2 tablespoons chopped parsley
Vegetable cooking spray

1. Make the Cilantro Sauce: Place a small skillet over medium-high until hot; add the cumin seeds, and cook, stirring constantly, 1 to 2 minutes or until toasted. Cool 10 minutes. Process the cilantro, next 4 ingredients, 2 tablespoons water, and toasted cumin seeds in a blender until smooth, stopping to scrape down sides as needed. Cover and chill until ready to serve.

2. Make the Mango-Red Onion Relish: Sauté the onion in 1 teaspoon hot olive oil in a small skillet over medium-high 6 to 8 minutes or until the onion is tender. Transfer to a medium bowl, and stir in the mango, next 3 ingredients, salt, and black pepper to taste.

3. Make the Beef Tenderloin: Rub steaks with 1 tablespoon olive oil. Sprinkle with 1 teaspoon salt and next 2 ingredients. Place a grill pan over medium-high until hot; cook the steaks 8 minutes on each side or to desired degree of doneness. Let stand 5 minutes. Thinly slice steak.

4. Make Herbed Cornbread Crostini: Preheat the oven to 450°F. Stir together the cornmeal mix and sugar in a large bowl; make a well in center of mixture. Whisk together the eggs, sour cream, buttermilk, and melted butter in a medium bowl. Add to the cornmeal mixture, stirring just until dry ingredients are moistened. Fold in the chopped chives and parsley. Spoon the batter into 3 lightly greased (with cooking spray) 12-cup muffin pans (about 1 tablespoon per cup), spreading the batter to cover bottoms of cups. Bake at 450°F for 8 minutes or until set. Immediately remove from pans to wire racks.

5. To assemble, top the flat sides of the Herbed Cornbread Crostini with relish and steak; drizzle with Cilantro Sauce.

Seafood St. Jacques, page 95

**Duxelles-Stuffed
Pork Tenderloin,
page 85**

**Veal Chops Milanese
with Lemon and Herbs, page 77**

**Braised Brisket with
Red Wine Reduction, page 88**

FESTIVE ENTRÉES

From comforting pot pies to classic centerpiece roasts, planning the holiday feast has never been easier.

CLASSIC ROASTED DUCK

The secret to crispy skin is a dry duck. Pat ducks thoroughly with a paper towel before, during, and after refrigerating. Store, uncovered, in the coldest part of your fridge up to two days ahead of cooking. This air-dries the skin for supercrisp results.

SERVES 8 to 10 · **HANDS-ON:** 30 minutes · **TOTAL:** 11 hours, 50 minutes

2 (6- to 7-pound) whole ducks
Kitchen string
2 teaspoons kosher salt
½ teaspoon freshly ground black pepper

1 cup orange marmalade
¼ cup bourbon
3 tablespoons molasses
1 tablespoon fresh lemon juice

¼ teaspoon ground ginger
¼ teaspoon dried crushed red pepper
Garnishes: grilled orange wedges, lemon leaves

1. Remove the giblets from the ducks, and reserve for another use. Rinse the ducks, and pat dry with paper towels. Remove the excess skin and fat. Tie the legs together with kitchen string; chill, uncovered, 10 to 48 hours.

2. Preheat the oven to 450°F. Line a jelly-roll pan with aluminum foil, and place a wire rack in the prepared pan. Let the ducks stand at room temperature 15 minutes. Prick the legs, thighs, and breasts with a fork. Rub the ducks with salt and black pepper, and place, breast side up, on the wire rack in the prepared pan. Bake at 450°F for 45 minutes.

3. Meanwhile, stir together the orange marmalade and next 5 ingredients in a small saucepan. Bring to a boil over high. Reduce heat to medium, and cook, stirring often, 10 to 15 minutes or until reduced to about 1 cup.

4. Remove the ducks from the oven, and carefully spoon the fat from the pan. Brush the ducks with the orange marmalade glaze. Reduce the oven temperature to 350°F, and bake at 350°F for 20 to 25 minutes or until a meat thermometer inserted in the thickest portion registers 180°F. Let stand 15 minutes before serving.

GINGER AND BROWN SUGAR SMOKED HOLIDAY HAM

This holiday ham will be a hit with its bright ginger and mellow brown sugar flavors.
There's plenty here to feed a crowd, but if you are hoping for leftovers
for sandwiches and meaty ham bone soup, there's plenty for that as well.

SERVES 12 · **HANDS-ON:** 13 minutes · **TOTAL:** 3 hours, 43 minutes

1 (15-pound) smoked fully cooked, bone-in ham

42 (¼- x ⅛-inch) crystallized ginger pieces

1½ cups firmly packed light brown sugar

¾ cup ginger ale

½ cup whole-grain mustard

2 tablespoons apple cider vinegar

1 tablespoon chopped fresh thyme

1. Preheat the oven to 325°F. Remove skin and excess fat from the ham. Make shallow cuts in the fat 1 inch apart in a diamond pattern. Make a small slit in the center of each diamond; insert ginger pieces into the slits.

2. Place the ham on a rack in a large roasting pan. Pour water into the roasting pan to a depth of ¼ inch. Cover the top of ham loosely with aluminum foil. Bake at 325°F for 2 hours and 40 minutes or until a meat thermometer inserted into thickest portion, not touching bone, registers 135°F. Remove ham from oven. Increase the oven temperature to 425°F.

3. Stir together the brown sugar and next 4 ingredients. Brush 1 cup brown sugar mixture over the ham. Bake, uncovered, at 425°F for 40 minutes or until glazed and brown, basting every 10 minutes with the remaining brown sugar mixture. Let stand 10 minutes before carving.

HEAVENLY HAM BONE SOUP

A leftover ham bone after the holiday meal is a gift in itself. Use this recipe to make the most of holiday leftovers and to create a comforting, filling soup for the coldest weeks of winter.

SERVES 10 · **HANDS-ON:** 10 minutes · **TOTAL:** 1 hour, 35 minutes

2 celery ribs, quartered
1 (3-pound) meaty ham bone
1 large carrot, halved
1 medium onion, halved
1 bay leaf
12 cups water
1 tablespoon olive oil
1 cup diced onion (from 1 onion)

½ cup carrots, diced (from 1 carrot)
½ cup celery, diced (from 1 rib)
4 large garlic cloves, minced
1 (14.5-ounce) can diced tomatoes, undrained

3 cups drained cooked butter beans, black-eyed peas, or pinto beans
2 cups drained cooked collard greens, turnip greens, or kale
1 cup water

1. Bring the first 5 ingredients and 12 cups water to a boil in a large stockpot; reduce heat, and simmer, uncovered, 1 hour. Remove the ham bone; cool completely. Pour the broth through a fine wire-mesh strainer into a large bowl. Reserve any pieces of the ham; discard the remaining solids.

2. Heat the olive oil in a Dutch oven over medium-high. Add the diced onion and next 3 ingredients; cook, stirring often, 5 to 6 minutes or until the vegetables are tender. Stir in the tomatoes, beans, greens, reserved ham, and 8 cups of the reserved broth; reserve the remaining broth for another use, or discard. Stir in 1 cup water. Bring to a boil; reduce heat, and simmer, uncovered, 20 minutes, stirring occasionally.

BOURBON-CIDER ROASTED TURKEY WITH BBQ GRAVY

Soaking your turkey overnight in this sweet brine will ensure tender, moist meat that is full of flavor. If you'd rather skip the barbecue flavor in your gravy, simply leave out the sauce.

SERVES 10 to 12 • **HANDS-ON:** 36 minutes • **TOTAL:** 11 hours, 56 minutes

6 cups water
1½ cups kosher salt
½ cup firmly packed light brown sugar
2 cups ice cubes
2 cups apple cider or apple juice
2 cups bourbon
1 tablespoon black peppercorns
1 (13-pound) whole fresh turkey

Vegetable cooking spray
¼ cup melted butter
2 tablespoons kosher salt
1 tablespoon onion powder
1 tablespoon garlic powder
1 tablespoon paprika
1 tablespoon chopped fresh sage
1 tablespoon chopped fresh thyme
1½ teaspoons freshly ground black pepper

1 tablespoon olive oil
½ cup chopped onion
3 garlic cloves, minced
⅓ cup all-purpose flour
1 to 1½ cups chicken stock
¼ cup barbecue sauce
½ teaspoon freshly ground black pepper

1. Bring 6 cups water to a boil in a large stockpot over medium-high. Stir in 1½ cups kosher salt and brown sugar. Reduce heat, and simmer, uncovered, 2 to 3 minutes or until the salt and sugar dissolve, stirring occasionally. Transfer to a large bowl; add the ice and next 3 ingredients. Let stand 30 minutes or until mixture cools to room temperature, stirring occasionally.

2. Remove and discard the giblets and neck from the turkey. Submerge the turkey in the cooled brine. Cover and chill 8 hours to overnight.

3. Grease a broiler pan and rack with cooking spray. Preheat the oven to 325°F. Remove the turkey from the brine, discarding the brine; drain well and pat dry. Tie ends of the legs together with string; tuck the wing tips under. Place the turkey, breast side up, on prepared pan. Brush the turkey with melted butter. Combine 2 tablespoons salt and next 7 ingredients in a small bowl; rub evenly over skin and inside cavity.

4. Bake, uncovered, at 325°F for 2 hours and 30 minutes to 3 hours or until a meat thermometer inserted into thickest portion of thigh registers 165°F. Cover loosely with aluminum foil, and let stand 25 minutes before carving.

5. Pour the pan drippings from the bottom of the broiler pan into a glass measuring cup, and let stand 5 minutes or until fat rises to top. Spoon ¼ cup fat from top of drippings, and reserve. Discard the remaining fat, reserving remaining drippings in measuring cup.

6. Heat ¼ cup reserved fat in a large saucepan over medium-high. Add the onion and garlic; sauté 3 minutes or until tender. Sprinkle the flour over onion mixture; cook, stirring constantly, 2 minutes. Add the reserved turkey drippings and enough chicken stock to measure 2 cups. Bring to a boil; reduce heat, and simmer 5 minutes or until thickened. Stir in the barbecue sauce and ½ teaspoon pepper. Serve the gravy with sliced turkey.

NOTE: We tested with Stubb's Original Barbecue Sauce.

ROASTED LEG OF LAMB WITH LEMON-HERB SALT

Leg of lamb is an easy yet holiday-worthy roast. Buzz together the flavorful herb seasoning in a food processor, and rub it onto the meat at least 12 hours before roasting. Trust an instant-read meat thermometer to ensure the lamb is the perfect rosy pink in the center.

SERVES 8 · **HANDS-ON:** 15 minutes · **TOTAL:** 14 hours, 50 minutes

⅓ **cup loosely packed fresh rosemary leaves**

⅓ **cup loosely packed fresh oregano leaves**

3 **teaspoons lemon zest**

¼ **cup kosher salt**

¼ **teaspoon freshly ground black pepper**

1 **(5- to 7-pound) bone-in leg of lamb, trimmed**

2 **tablespoons olive oil**

Garnish: roasted vegetables

1. Process first 5 ingredients in a food processor 2 to 3 minutes or until blended. Rub the herb mixture over the lamb, and place on a rack in a roasting pan. Chill 12 to 24 hours.

2. Let the lamb stand at room temperature 30 minutes. Meanwhile, preheat oven to 450°F. Brush the lamb with olive oil.

3. Bake at 450°F for 45 minutes; reduce oven temperature to 350°F, and bake 1 more hour or until a meat thermometer inserted into the thickest portion registers 145°F. Let the lamb stand 20 minutes before serving.

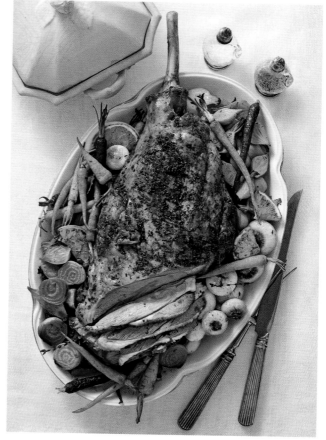

VEAL CHOPS MILANESE WITH LEMON AND HERBS

Ask your butcher to "french" the chops for you so you take home clean meat that's ready to prep.

SERVES 6 · **HANDS-ON:** 45 minutes · **TOTAL:** 1 hour

6   (6- to 7-ounce) frenched veal chops
2½ cups panko (Japanese-style breadcrumbs)
½   cup freshly grated Parmigiano-Reggiano cheese
2   tablespoons fresh rosemary leaves

2   tablespoons fresh thyme leaves
1   teaspoon lemon zest
2   large eggs
1   tablespoon water
2   tablespoons kosher salt
1½ teaspoons freshly ground black pepper

¾   cup olive oil
3   ounces (6 tablespoons) butter
Garnishes: fresh flat-leaf parsley leaves and sprigs, lemon slices

1. Preheat the oven to 400°F. Place each veal chop between 2 sheets of heavy-duty plastic wrap, and flatten to ¼-inch thickness, using a rolling pin or the flat side of a meat mallet.

2. Process the panko, Parmigiano-Reggiano cheese, rosemary leaves, thyme leaves, and lemon zest in a food processor until the herbs are finely chopped. Transfer the panko mixture to a shallow dish.

3. Whisk together the eggs and 1 tablespoon water in another shallow dish. Sprinkle each veal chop with 1 teaspoon of the kosher salt and ¼ teaspoon of the pepper. Dip each chop in the egg mixture, shaking off excess. (Do not dip the bone.) Dredge the chops in the panko mixture, pressing to adhere.

4. Cook 1 chop in 2 tablespoons of the hot olive oil and 1 tablespoon of the butter in a large skillet over medium 2 minutes on each side or until golden brown. Repeat the procedure with the remaining chops, oil, and butter, wiping the skillet clean after each chop. Place the chops on wire racks in 2 jelly-roll pans.

5. Bake at 400°F for 15 minutes. Serve immediately.

GRILLED CORNISH HENS WITH HERB BRINE

If you don't own kitchen or poultry shears, that's ok—a pair of clean, heavy-duty scissors will work just as well for cutting up the Cornish hens.

SERVES 6 to 8 • **HANDS-ON:** 45 minutes • **TOTAL:** 11 hours

3 tablespoons kosher salt
1½ teaspoons freshly ground black pepper
½ teaspoon garlic powder
½ teaspoon onion powder

2 tablespoons fresh thyme leaves
2 tablespoons fresh flat-leaf parsley leaves

6 (20-ounce) Cornish hens
Parchment paper
Garnish: fresh thyme sprigs

1. Process the first 6 ingredients in a food processor 15 to 20 seconds or until well combined.

2. Pat the hens dry with paper towels. Place each hen, breast side down, on a cutting board. Cut the hens, using kitchen shears, along both sides of the backbone, separating the backbone from the hen. Discard the bone. Open the hens as you would a book; turn breast side up, and press firmly against breastbone with the heel of your hand until bone cracks. Tuck the wing tips under. Place the hens in a parchment paper-lined jelly-roll pan.

3. Sprinkle the salt mixture over the hens, and chill, uncovered, 10 to 24 hours.

4. Preheat the grill to 350° to 400°F (medium-high). Grill the hens, skin side down and covered with grill lid, 8 minutes on each side or until a meat thermometer inserted in the thickest portion registers 165°F. Remove from the grill, and let stand 5 minutes.

SPICE-RUBBED TENDERLOIN WITH MUSTARD-CREAM SAUCE

*Since beef tenderloin doesn't have much fat, it can easily become dry and overcooked.
For tender slices, don't cook past a meat thermometer registering 130°F in the center.*

SERVES 10 to 12 · **HANDS-ON:** 15 minutes · **TOTAL:** 1 hour, 50 minutes, including sauce

SPICE-RUBBED TENDERLOIN:
Vegetable cooking spray
2½ teaspoons kosher salt
1 teaspoon freshly ground black pepper
1 teaspoon dried thyme
1 teaspoon garlic powder
½ teaspoon ground cumin
½ teaspoon paprika
½ teaspoon ground red pepper

1 (5- to 6-pound) beef tenderloin, trimmed
1 tablespoon olive oil

MUSTARD-CREAM SAUCE:
1 shallot, minced (about 3 tablespoons)
1 tablespoon olive oil
1 garlic clove, minced
1 cup dry white wine

¼ cup Creole mustard
2 teaspoons sugar
1 (8-ounce) container sour cream
1 teaspoon kosher salt
¼ teaspoon freshly ground black pepper
Garnish: fresh sage leaves

1. Make the Spice-Rubbed Tenderloin: Preheat the oven to 500°F. Lightly grease a wire rack with cooking spray, and place in a roasting pan. Stir together the kosher salt and next 6 ingredients. Rub the tenderloin evenly with the olive oil. Sprinkle the salt mixture over the tenderloin, pressing to adhere. Cover and let stand at room temperature 30 minutes. Place the tenderloin on the prepared pan.

2. Bake at 500°F for 15 minutes; reduce the oven temperature to 375°F, and bake 25 to 30 minutes or until a meat thermometer inserted in the thickest portion registers 130°F (for medium-rare) or to desired degree of doneness. Remove from the oven; let stand 10 minutes before slicing.

3. Make the Mustard-Cream Sauce: Sauté the shallot in hot oil in a medium skillet over medium 2 minutes or until soft; add the garlic, and sauté 1 minute. Stir in the wine, mustard, and sugar; bring to a boil. Cook, stirring constantly, 3 minutes or until the mixture has thickened and is reduced by about half. Remove from heat, and whisk in the sour cream, salt, and pepper. Serve immediately with the tenderloin.

SHORT RIB POT PIES

To save time, buy already cooked short ribs in the refrigerated section of some warehouse stores; heat, and shred.

SERVES 6 · HANDS-ON: 47 minutes · TOTAL: 3 hours, 47 minutes

2 pounds boneless beef short ribs
1¾ teaspoons fine sea salt
1⅛ teaspoons freshly ground black pepper
2 tablespoons olive oil
2 cups dry red wine
1 cup shallots, halved (3 large shallots)

3 large garlic cloves, halved
2 sprigs fresh thyme
4 cups beef stock
1½ cups sliced carrots (3 carrots)
1½ cups sliced parsnips (2 parsnips)
1 (8-ounce) package fresh cremini mushrooms, quartered

1½ (17.3-ounce) packages frozen puff pastry sheets, thawed
¼ cup (1 ounce) all-purpose flour
¼ cup heavy cream
1 cup sour cream
2 tablespoons prepared horseradish
Garnish: fresh thyme leaves

1. Preheat the oven to 300°F. Rub the ribs with 1½ teaspoons of the salt and 1 teaspoon of the pepper. Cook the ribs, in 2 batches, in hot oil in an ovenproof Dutch oven over medium-high 2 minutes on each side or until brown. Remove the ribs from the Dutch oven.

2. Add the wine and next 3 ingredients to the Dutch oven. Bring to a boil; reduce heat, and simmer, uncovered, 10 minutes or until the mixture is reduced by half. Stir in the stock; simmer, uncovered, 5 minutes. Add the ribs; bake, covered, at 300°F for 2 hours. Turn the ribs over; add the carrots, parsnips, and mushrooms; bake, covered, 1 more hour or until ribs are tender. Remove from the oven.

3. Increase the oven temperature to 425°F. Unfold the pastry sheets on a lightly floured surface. Cut each pastry sheet into 4 circles, using a 4-inch cutter. Place on an ungreased baking sheet. Bake at 425°F for 18 minutes or until golden brown and puffed. Remove the centers from the circles. Keep warm.

4. Remove the ribs from the cooking liquid, reserving cooking liquid. Place the meat in a large bowl; separate into chunks with 2 forks.

5. Pour the cooking liquid through a fine wire-mesh strainer into a bowl. Discard the thyme, reserving the vegetable mixture. Bring 2 cups of the strained liquid to a boil in a medium saucepan, reserving the remaining liquid for another use. Combine the flour and heavy cream in a small bowl, whisking until smooth. Whisk the flour mixture into broth. Cook, whisking constantly, until thickened and smooth. Stir in the reserved vegetables and rib meat. Cook 2 minutes or until thoroughly heated, whisking occasionally.

6. Combine sour cream, horseradish, remaining ¼ teaspoon salt, and remaining ⅛ teaspoon pepper.

7. Place pastry shells on a serving platter. Spoon meat mixture evenly into shells. Top each with a dollop of sour cream mixture, and garnish with fresh thyme, if desired. Serve immediately.

DUXELLES-STUFFED PORK TENDERLOIN

Pork tenderloins are delicious when stuffed with this classic sautéed mushroom mixture. Wrapping in prosciutto ensures a moist interior while a rich Marsala cream sauce makes this an extra-special, holiday-worthy main attraction.

SERVES 8 to 10 · **HANDS-ON:** 45 minutes · **TOTAL:** 1 hour, 15 minutes

Vegetable cooking spray
2 shallots, chopped
2 tablespoons olive oil
2 (4-ounce) packages assorted mushrooms, coarsely chopped
1¼ teaspoons kosher salt
1¼ teaspoons freshly ground black pepper

2 large garlic cloves, minced
1½ teaspoons chopped fresh thyme
¼ cup chopped fresh parsley
½ teaspoon firmly packed lemon zest
2 tablespoons fine, dry breadcrumbs
2 (1¼-pounds) pork tenderloins

1 (4-ounce) package thinly sliced prosciutto
Kitchen string
½ cup Marsala wine
1 cup reduced-sodium fat-free chicken broth
¾ cup heavy cream
Garnish: fresh thyme sprigs

1. Lightly grease a roasting pan with cooking spray. Sauté the shallots in hot olive oil in a large nonstick skillet over medium 2 minutes or until crisp-tender. Add the mushrooms, ½ teaspoon of the salt, and ½ teaspoon of the pepper; sauté 7 minutes or until tender and liquid evaporates. Add the garlic and thyme; sauté 1 minute. Remove from heat, and stir in the parsley, lemon zest, and breadcrumbs. Cool completely.

2. Butterfly each tenderloin by making a horizontal cut into 1 side of pork, cutting to within ½ inch of other side. (Do not cut all the way through tenderloins.)

3. Unfold the tenderloins, forming rectangles, and place each between 2 sheets of heavy-duty plastic wrap; flatten to ½-inch thickness using a rolling pin or the flat side of a meat mallet.

4. Preheat the oven to 400°F. Spread the mushroom mixture evenly over the tenderloins, leaving a ½-inch border. Roll up the tenderloins, starting at 1 long side. Sprinkle the tenderloins with ½ teaspoon of the salt and ½ teaspoon of the pepper. Place half of the prosciutto, overlapping slices, on top of each tenderloin. Wrap the prosciutto around the tenderloins; secure with kitchen string at 2-inch intervals.

5. Place the tenderloins in the prepared pan. Bake, uncovered, at 400°F for 30 minutes or until a meat thermometer inserted into thickest portion registers 145°F.

6. Transfer the tenderloins to a platter, and cover with aluminum foil. Let stand 10 minutes.

7. Meanwhile, bring the Marsala to a boil in a medium saucepan over medium-high. Boil, uncovered, 6 minutes or until reduced by half, stirring occasionally. Stir in the chicken broth; return to a boil. Reduce heat, and simmer 9 minutes or until reduced by half. Stir in the heavy cream, and simmer 3 minutes or until slightly thickened. Stir in the remaining ¼ teaspoon salt and remaining ¼ teaspoon pepper. Serve the sauce with the pork.

MEATLOAF MUFFINS WITH MASHED-POTATO TOPS

If your family members are cheese lovers, top the potatoes with shredded cheese before baking.

SERVES 12 · **HANDS-ON:** 32 minutes · **TOTAL:** 1 hour, 17 minutes

MEATLOAF:
Vegetable cooking spray
1½ tablespoons olive oil
1 large onion, finely chopped (¾ cup)
1 to 2 carrots, finely chopped (¾ cup)
3 garlic cloves, minced
2¼ pounds extra-lean ground beef
1½ cups finely crushed bacon-flavored round buttery crackers (27 crackers)

¾ cup ketchup
1 teaspoon table salt
2 teaspoons Worcestershire sauce
¾ teaspoon chopped fresh oregano
½ teaspoon freshly ground black pepper
3 large eggs, beaten

MASHED POTATOES:
1½ pounds Yukon Gold potatoes, peeled and cut into 1-inch cubes (about 6 cups)
½ cup heavy cream, warmed
½ teaspoon table salt
2 ounces Parmesan cheese, shaved
1 ounce (2 tablespoons) butter, melted

1. Make the meatloaf: Preheat the oven to 350°F. Lightly grease 12 muffin cups with cooking spray. Heat the oil in a large nonstick skillet over medium-high. Add the onion and carrot; sauté 4 minutes. Add the garlic; sauté 1 minute. Remove from heat, and cool completely (15 minutes).

2. Combine the ground beef, crackers, next 6 ingredients, and carrot mixture in a large bowl, using hands.

3. Spoon about ½ cup beef mixture into each prepared muffin cup. Bake at 350°F for 35 minutes or until a meat thermometer inserted in the center registers 160°F. Remove the meatloaves from the oven. Increase the oven temperature to broil.

4. Meanwhile, make the mashed potatoes: Cook the potatoes in boiling, salted water to cover 15 minutes or until tender; drain. Press the potatoes through a ricer into a bowl. Stir in the cream and next 2 ingredients until smooth.

5. Insert a large metal star tip into a large decorating bag; fill with the mashed potato mixture. Pipe the potato mixture evenly onto the meatloaves; drizzle with the melted butter. Broil 6 minutes or until the potato is golden brown. Remove from the oven, and cool 5 minutes before serving.

SWEET-AND-SOUR CHICKEN WITH RICE

Crispy chicken bathed in a sweet sauce is a magnet for kids.
If bell peppers are not a family favorite, substitute steamed broccoli.

SERVES 4 · **HANDS-ON:** 28 minutes · **TOTAL:** 28 minutes

Canola oil
1 cup (4.5 ounces) all-purpose flour
½ teaspoon garlic powder
¼ teaspoon table salt
1 cup club soda
3 skinned and boned chicken thighs (½ pound), cut into 2-inch pieces
1 skinned and boned chicken breast (½ pound), cut into 2-inch pieces

2 tablespoons firmly packed light brown sugar
2 teaspoons cornstarch
½ cup canned pineapple juice
½ cup reduced-sodium fat-free chicken broth
6 tablespoons ketchup
5 tablespoons rice vinegar
2 tablespoons soy sauce
½ cup onion, cut into 1-inch pieces

1 red bell pepper, cut into 1-inch pieces
1 green bell pepper, cut into 1-inch pieces
2 teaspoons dark sesame oil
2 garlic cloves, minced
1½ cups (¾-inch) pieces fresh pineapple
2 cups hot cooked jasmine rice

1. Preheat the oven to 200°F. Pour oil to a depth of 3 inches into a Dutch oven; heat to 375°F.

2. Combine the flour, garlic powder, and salt in a medium bowl; make a well in center of mixture. Add the club soda to the flour mixture, stirring just until moistened.

3. Dip the chicken pieces into the batter, shaking off excess. Fry the chicken, in 2 batches, 2 minutes on each side or until golden brown. Drain on paper towels. Transfer to a baking sheet; keep warm in 200°F oven.

4. Combine the brown sugar and cornstarch in a bowl; stir in the pineapple juice and next 4 ingredients.

5. Sauté the onion and bell peppers in hot sesame oil in a large skillet over medium-high 4 minutes or until crisp-tender. Add the garlic; sauté 1 minute. Reduce heat to medium. Stir in the cornstarch mixture and fresh pineapple. Bring to a boil; cook, stirring constantly, 1 minute or until thickened. Add the chicken, stirring gently to coat. Serve over rice.

BRAISED BRISKET WITH RED WINE REDUCTION

During the chaos of the holiday season, this simple braise is the ideal make-ahead dish that becomes more flavorful the longer it stands. If desired, return the brisket slices and finished reduction to a Dutch oven or 3-quart glass dish; cover and chill until ready to reheat and serve.

SERVES 6 · **HANDS-ON:** 1 hour, 9 minutes · **TOTAL:** 4 hours, 59 minutes

1 tablespoon kosher salt
2 teaspoons freshly ground black pepper
2 teaspoons granulated garlic
1 (3¼-pound) beef brisket, trimmed
1 (750-milliliter) bottle Cabernet Sauvignon or other dry red wine

1 medium leek
2 tablespoons canola oil
1 large carrot, cut into 1-inch pieces
1 large celery rib, cut into 1-inch pieces
2 shallots, sliced
5 garlic cloves, crushed
4 flat-leaf parsley sprigs

7 fresh thyme sprigs
3 bay leaves
1 quart low-sodium beef stock
2 ounces (¼ cup) butter, softened
¼ cup (1.1 ounces) all-purpose flour
Garnish: fresh thyme leaves

1. Preheat the oven to 300°F. Combine the first 3 ingredients. Rub both sides of the brisket with the salt mixture.

2. Bring the red wine to a boil over medium-high in a medium saucepan; cook, uncovered, 14 minutes or until reduced to 1⅔ cups.

3. Meanwhile, remove and discard root end and dark green top of leek. Cut in half lengthwise, and rinse thoroughly under cold running water to remove grit and sand. Drain. Cut into 1-inch pieces.

4. Cook the brisket in 1 tablespoon of the hot oil in an ovenproof Dutch oven over medium-high 4 minutes on each side or until well browned. Remove the brisket from Dutch oven. Heat remaining 1 tablespoon oil in Dutch oven. Add the leek, carrot, and next 6 ingredients; sauté 3 minutes or until lightly browned. Add the reduced red wine and beef stock, stirring to loosen browned bits from bottom of Dutch oven. Return the brisket to Dutch oven.

5. Bake, covered, at 300°F for 3 hours and 30 minutes or until tender, turning halfway through.

6. Transfer the brisket to a platter, reserving the cooking liquid in Dutch oven; cover and keep warm. Let the cooking liquid stand 20 minutes. Skim and discard the fat from the cooking liquid; bring to a simmer in Dutch oven over medium-high. Simmer, uncovered, 28 minutes or until reduced to 5 cups. Pour liquid through a fine wire-mesh strainer into a bowl, pressing with the back of a wooden spoon to release liquid. Discard the solids.

7. Return the liquid to the Dutch oven; bring to a boil. Stir together the butter and flour in a small bowl until a paste forms. Whisk the butter mixture into the boiling liquid, whisking until smooth. Reduce heat, and simmer 5 minutes or until thickened. Cut the brisket across the grain into thin slices using a sharp knife. Serve with the red wine sauce.

LASAGNA BOLOGNESE

This luscious pasta dish is well worth the effort. Traditional lasagna Bolognese includes homemade spinach lasagna noodles, but we've taken a shortcut here with dried noodles. The Bolognese sauce may be prepared up to two days in advance.

SERVES 12 • **HANDS-ON:** 40 minutes • **TOTAL:** 3 hours, 44 minutes

2   tablespoons olive oil
2   large onions, finely chopped
     (1¼ cups)
1 to 2 celery ribs, finely chopped
     (¾ cup)
1 to 2 carrots, finely chopped
     (¾ cup)
3   garlic cloves, minced
1   pound ground chuck
½   pound mild Italian sausage,
     casings removed

¼   cup tomato paste
2   (28-ounce) cans
     crushed tomatoes
½   teaspoon freshly ground
     black pepper
4   cups milk
2½   teaspoons kosher salt
     Vegetable cooking spray
16   uncooked lasagna noodles
     Olive oil

3   ounces (6 tablespoons) butter
6   tablespoons (1½ ounces)
     all-purpose flour
⅛   teaspoon freshly
     grated nutmeg
2½   cups (10 ounces) freshly
     grated Parmigiano-Reggiano
     cheese

1. Heat the oil in a Dutch oven over medium. Add the onion and next 3 ingredients; sauté 8 minutes or until vegetables are crisp-tender. Add the beef and sausage; increase heat to medium-high, and cook, stirring often, 6 to 8 minutes or until meat crumbles and is well browned. Stir in the tomato paste; cook 2 minutes. Stir in the tomatoes, pepper, 1 cup of the milk, and 2 teaspoons of the salt; bring to a simmer. Reduce heat to low, and simmer 1 hour and 30 minutes or until sauce is thickened and reduced to 9 cups, stirring occasionally.

2. Lightly grease a 13- x 9-inch baking dish with cooking spray. Prepare the noodles according to package directions. Drain and plunge into cold water to stop the cooking process; drain and layer on a baking sheet. Drizzle olive oil between layers to prevent noodles from sticking together.

3. Melt the butter in a heavy medium saucepan over low; add the flour, whisking until smooth. Cook, whisking constantly, 1 minute. Gradually whisk in remaining 3 cups milk; cook, whisking constantly, over medium 2 minutes or until thickened and bubbly. Add the nutmeg, ½ cup of the cheese, and remaining ½ teaspoon salt; cook, stirring constantly, until cheese melts and sauce is smooth. Remove from heat.

4. Preheat the oven to 375°F. Spread about 1¾ cups Bolognese sauce in bottom of the prepared dish. Layer 4 lasagna noodles over sauce. Top with about 1¾ cups of the Bolognese sauce, a scant 1 cup of the white sauce, and ½ cup of the cheese. Repeat layers 3 times, beginning with the noodles and ending with the cheese. Coat the dull side of a large piece of aluminum foil with cooking spray. Cover the casserole tightly with prepared foil, coated side down.

5. Bake at 375° for 40 minutes. Uncover and bake 20 more minutes or until the noodles are tender and the top is browned. Let stand 20 minutes before serving.

SHRIMP AND GOUDA GRITS

Using the rendered fat from the sausage to sauté the vegetables lends a smoky, spicy flavor to this beloved Lowcountry dish.

SERVES 8 · **HANDS-ON:** 47 minutes · **TOTAL:** 47 minutes, including grits

SHRIMP:
8 ounces andouille sausage, sliced
1 medium onion, chopped
1 medium-size red bell pepper, chopped
1 medium-size green bell pepper, chopped
4 garlic cloves, minced
2 pounds medium-size raw shrimp, peeled and deveined

2 teaspoons Creole seasoning
2 tablespoons all-purpose flour
1 cup chicken broth
½ cup dry white wine

GOUDA GRITS:
4 cups chicken broth
3½ cups milk
2 teaspoons table salt

½ teaspoon freshly ground black pepper
2 cups uncooked quick-cooking grits
6 ounces Gouda cheese, shredded
2 ounces (¼ cup) butter
¼ cup chopped fresh parsley

1. Make the shrimp: Cook the sausage in a large skillet over medium-high 6 minutes or until browned. Remove from the skillet with a slotted spoon. Add the onion and peppers to pan; sauté 5 to 8 minutes or until tender. Add the garlic; sauté 30 seconds. Stir in the shrimp; sprinkle with Creole seasoning and flour, tossing to coat. Gradually stir in the chicken broth and wine. Cook, stirring often, 4 minutes or until the shrimp turn pink and the sauce is slightly thickened. Stir in the cooked sausage.

2. Make Gouda Grits: Bring 4 cups of broth and the next 3 ingredients to a boil in a Dutch oven over medium. Gradually whisk in the grits. Reduce heat, and simmer, uncovered, 10 minutes or until thick, whisking often. Remove from heat; stir in the cheese and butter, whisking until the cheese melts. Serve the shrimp over the grits. Sprinkle with fresh parsley.

SEAFOOD ST. JACQUES

Sweet shrimp and scallops in a velvety sauce are traditionally presented in beautiful scallop shells, but individual gratin dishes work just as well. This make-ahead dish can be popped under the broiler after an evening candlelight service. Round out the meal with crusty French bread and a green salad. It's perfect served with dry Champagne for holiday toasting.

SERVES 8 • **HANDS-ON:** 20 minutes • **TOTAL:** 25 minutes

Vegetable cooking spray
1   pound sea scallops (about 20 scallops)
4   ounces (½ cup) butter
2   tablespoons finely chopped shallots
1   tablespoon finely chopped garlic
1   (8-ounce) package fresh mushrooms, thinly sliced

½   teaspoon table salt
¼   teaspoon freshly ground black pepper
1   cup dry white wine
1   pound medium-size raw shrimp, peeled and deveined
¼   cup (1.1 ounces) all-purpose flour
1   cup seafood stock
1   cup heavy cream

½   teaspoon hot sauce, or to taste
2   tablespoons finely chopped fresh parsley
⅛   teaspoon ground red pepper
1   cup panko (Japanese-style breadcrumbs)
¼   cup grated fresh Parmesan cheese

1. Lightly grease 8 (10-ounce) gratin dishes with cooking spray. Place dishes on a large baking sheet. Rinse the scallops, and pat dry. Melt 3 tablespoons of the butter in a large skillet over medium-high. Add the shallots, garlic, and mushrooms; sauté 3 to 4 minutes or until tender. Stir in the salt, pepper, and wine. Add the scallops and shrimp; cover and cook 3 to 4 minutes or until shrimp turn pink and scallops are done. Transfer the seafood and mushrooms to a bowl using a slotted spoon; reserve cooking liquid in skillet.

2. Add ¼ cup of the butter to the reserved cooking liquid; cook over medium-high, whisking until butter melts. Whisk in the flour until smooth. Add the seafood stock, cream, and hot sauce; cook, whisking constantly, 5 minutes or until the sauce is thickened. Remove from the heat. Cool slightly.

3. Preheat the broiler with the oven rack 8 inches from heat. Divide the seafood mixture evenly among the prepared dishes. Spoon about ⅓ cup sauce over the seafood mixture in each dish.

4. Place remaining 1 tablespoon butter in a medium microwave-safe bowl. Cover and microwave at HIGH 1 minute or until butter melts. Stir in the parsley and red pepper. Add the panko and cheese; toss well. Sprinkle crumb mixture evenly over the gratin dishes.

5. Broil 4 minutes or until the sauce is bubbly and tops are browned and crisp. Serve immediately.

MAKE-AHEAD: Cover and chill the filled dishes up to 1 day ahead. Remove from the refrigerator, and let stand 20 minutes. Sprinkle with the crumb topping, and broil as directed in recipe.

SEARED SCALLOPS WITH LEMON-PARMESAN DRIZZLE

Scallops may not be your idea of a traditional holiday dinner, but these seared scallops are sure to change that impression. It's an elegant main dish that's simple and delicious.

SERVES 8 • **HANDS-ON:** 15 minutes • **TOTAL:** 23 minutes

2½ **pounds sea scallops (45 scallops)**
½ **teaspoon kosher salt**
¼ **teaspoon freshly ground black pepper**
2 **tablespoons olive oil**
½ **cup dry white wine**

½ **teaspoon firmly packed lemon zest**
1 **teaspoon lemon juice**
1 **small shallot, minced**
1 **garlic clove, minced**
4 **ounces (½ cup) cold butter, cut up**

1 **ounce Parmesan cheese, grated**
1 **tablespoon heavy cream**
Garnishes: lemon wedges, chopped fresh parsley

1. Rinse the scallops, and pat dry with paper towels; sprinkle with salt and pepper.

2. Heat the olive oil in a large skillet over medium-high; add one-third of the scallops, and cook 3 minutes or until golden brown. Turn over; cook 1 more minute. Remove from skillet; cover loosely with aluminum foil, and keep warm. Repeat procedure twice with the remaining scallops.

3. Bring the wine and next 4 ingredients to a boil in a small saucepan over medium-high. Reduce heat, and simmer, uncovered, 8 minutes or until liquid almost evaporates. Add the butter, 1 piece at a time, whisking until melted and smooth after each addition. Remove from heat; whisk in the cheese and cream.

4. Arrange the scallops on a large serving platter. Drizzle with the sauce. Serve immediately.

Harvest Salad with Roasted Citrus Vinaigrette and Spiced Pecans, page 104

Roasted Garlic Duchess Potatoes, page 117

Gnocchi Mac and Cheese, page 100
Fontina-Chive Yorkshire Puddings, page 101

Brussels Sprouts with Parmesan Cream, page 107

ALL THE TRIMMINGS

Side dishes are often the stars of the Southern table and these showstoppers are no exception.

GNOCCHI MAC AND CHEESE

Make this kid-friendly side an elegant entrée by serving with a salad and warm, crusty bread.

SERVES 6 to 8 · **HANDS-ON:** 30 minutes · **TOTAL:** 1 hour

Vegetable cooking spray

3 quarts water

2 (16-ounce) packages potato gnocchi

¼ cup plus 2½ teaspoons kosher salt

3 tablespoons butter

2 shallots, finely chopped

3 tablespoons all-purpose flour

2 tablespoons fresh thyme leaves, finely chopped

2½ cups milk

2 tablespoons Dijon mustard

¼ teaspoon hot sauce

4 ounces sharp Cheddar cheese, grated

4 ounces extra-sharp white Cheddar cheese, grated

1. Preheat the oven to 375°F. Lightly grease an 11- x 7-inch or a 2-quart baking dish with cooking spray. Bring 3 quarts water to a boil in a stockpot or large saucepan. Add both packages of the gnocchi and ¼ cup of the kosher salt. Boil about 3 minutes or until the gnocchi float.

2. Melt the butter in a large saucepan over medium. Add the shallots, and sauté 30 seconds or until fragrant. Add the flour and chopped thyme, and cook, stirring constantly, 2 to 3 minutes or until mixture is golden brown. Gradually whisk in the milk. Increase heat to high.

3. Bring the mixture to a boil, whisking occasionally. Reduce heat to medium-low, and simmer, whisking constantly, 5 minutes or until slightly thickened and mixture coats the back of a spoon. Stir in the mustard and hot sauce. Remove from heat.

4. Add the sharp and extra-sharp Cheddar cheeses, and stir until melted. Stir in the gnocchi and remaining 2½ teaspoons salt, and transfer to the prepared baking dish.

5. Bake at 375°F for 25 minutes or until the gnocchi is puffed and sauce is golden and bubbly. Increase the oven temperature to broil, and broil 2 minutes or until the top is slightly browned. Let stand 5 minutes, and serve immediately.

NOTE: We tested with Gia Russa Gnocchi with Potato.

FONTINA-CHIVE YORKSHIRE PUDDINGS

Don't skip the first step: For the fluffiest, puffiest puddings, make sure the muffin pan is super hot. You can also make these in popover pans.

SERVES 8 to 10 · **HANDS-ON:** 25 minutes · **TOTAL:** 55 minutes

6 bacon slices, finely chopped
1½ cups (6.75 ounces) all-purpose flour
1 teaspoon kosher salt

4 large eggs
1¾ cups milk
4 ounces grated fontina cheese

2 tablespoons thinly sliced fresh chives
Garnish: sliced fresh chives

1. Preheat the oven to 450°F. Heat a 12-cup muffin pan in the oven 15 minutes.

2. Meanwhile, cook the bacon in a medium skillet over medium, stirring occasionally, 8 to 9 minutes or until crisp. Remove the bacon, using a slotted spoon, and drain on paper towels. Reserve drippings.

3. Whisk together the flour and kosher salt in a large bowl. Whisk together the eggs and milk in a medium bowl. Gently whisk the egg mixture into the flour mixture until well blended. Stir the cheese, chives, and cooked bacon into the flour-egg mixture.

4. Spoon 1 teaspoon of the bacon drippings into each cup of the hot muffin pan; place muffin pan in oven for 2 minutes. Carefully remove pan. Divide the batter evenly among cups.

5. Bake at 450°F for 25 minutes or until puffed and golden brown. (Center will still be wet.) Serve immediately.

Gnocchi Mac and Cheese

Fontina-Chive
Yorkshire Puddings

CHRISTMAS SALAD

*A warm vinaigrette softens these sturdy greens, but their structure will hold
up for two hours on a holiday buffet. Prep all the ingredients ahead, and store
in individual zip-top plastic freezer bags in your refrigerator until ready to toss with the
warm vinaigrette. We love the candy-striped interiors of Chioggia beets for this recipe.*

SERVES 8 to 10 • **HANDS-ON:** 20 minutes • **TOTAL:** 20 minutes

8 ounces thick bacon, coarsely chopped

1 cup sliced red onion

1½ teaspoons kosher salt

¾ teaspoon freshly ground black pepper

½ cup red wine vinegar

2 tablespoons honey

1 bunch Lacinato kale, stemmed and coarsely chopped (about 7 cups loosely packed)

1 bunch red Swiss chard, stemmed and coarsely chopped (about 8 cups loosely packed)

2 small beets, thinly sliced

½ cup toasted pumpkin seeds

½ cup dried cherries

½ cup crumbled feta cheese

1. Cook the bacon in a large skillet over medium, stirring occasionally, 6 to 8 minutes or until crisp; remove the bacon, using a slotted spoon, and drain on paper towels. Reserve 6 tablespoons of the drippings in skillet. Add the onion, ½ teaspoon of the salt, and ¼ teaspoon of the pepper, and sauté 2 minutes. Remove from heat.

2. Add the red wine vinegar to skillet, and stir to loosen browned bits from bottom of skillet. Whisk in the honey.

3. Toss together the chopped kale, Swiss chard, onion mixture, remaining 1 teaspoon salt, and remaining ½ teaspoon black pepper in a large bowl. Transfer to a serving platter. Top with the cooked bacon, beet slices, pumpkin seeds, dried cherries, and feta cheese. Serve immediately.

HARVEST SALAD WITH ROASTED CITRUS VINAIGRETTE AND SPICED PECANS

Grainy Creole mustard adds texture and a delightful kick to the dressing, and roasting the lemons and oranges heightens both the sweet and sour flavors, creating a wonderfully nuanced balance. If you can find satsuma oranges, definitely use them to add a bright, sunshiny tang. You can make the vinaigrette and pecans several days ahead.

SERVES 6 to 8 • **HANDS-ON:** 20 minutes • **TOTAL:** 50 minutes

SPICED GLAZED PECANS:
- ¼ cup sugar
- ¼ teaspoon ground cinnamon
- ¼ teaspoon ground ginger
- ⅛ teaspoon ground cloves
- 1 cup coarsely chopped pecans
- Vegetable cooking spray
- Wax paper

HARVEST SALAD WITH ROASTED CITRUS VINAIGRETTE:
- 1 lemon, halved, bottoms trimmed flat
- 1 medium-size orange or 2 satsuma oranges, halved
- 1 tablespoon sugar
- 1 tablespoon sherry vinegar
- 2 tablespoons Creole mustard
- 2 teaspoons honey
- 1 garlic clove, minced

- Kosher salt
- Freshly ground black pepper
- ⅔ cup extra virgin olive oil
- 6 cups packed mixed bitter greens (such as frisée, radicchio, and arugula)
- 1 small red onion, thinly sliced
- 1 red-skinned apple or pear, thinly sliced
- 2 ounces crumbled Gorgonzola or other blue cheese

1. Make the pecans: Combine the first 4 ingredients in a heavy saucepan over medium. Add the pecans, and cook, stirring constantly, 7 minutes or until sugar melts and coats pecans. Spread on greased (with cooking spray) wax paper, and cool.

2. Make the salad: Preheat the broiler with the oven rack 3 to 5 inches from heat. Line a jelly-roll pan with aluminum foil. Pat the lemon and orange halves dry with a paper towel, and sprinkle cut sides with sugar. Place, cut side up, in the prepared pan, and broil 5 to 8 minutes or until caramelized and slightly softened. Cool in pan on a wire rack 10 minutes.

3. Squeeze the juice from the broiled citrus into a small bowl. Stir in the vinegar and next 3 ingredients. Add salt and pepper to taste. Let citrus mixture stand 10 minutes. Add the oil in a slow, steady stream, whisking constantly until smooth.

4. Toss together the greens, onion slices, and apple slices with desired amount of vinaigrette in a large bowl. Cover and refrigerate any remaining dressing to use later (up to 1 week). Season the salad with salt and pepper, and toss again. Sprinkle with the cheese and glazed pecans.

Brussels Sprouts
with Parmesan Cream

BRUSSELS SPROUTS WITH PARMESAN CREAM

For the most tender Brussels sprouts, look in the produce section for sprouts sold on the stalk. Cut sprouts from the stalk and store in a plastic freezer bag in the crisper drawer of your fridge.

SERVES 6 to 8 · **HANDS-ON:** 25 minutes · **TOTAL:** 50 minutes

3 **pounds fresh Brussels sprouts**
1½ **tablespoons olive oil**
2 **teaspoons kosher salt**
½ **teaspoon freshly ground black pepper**

2 **cups heavy cream**
3 **fresh rosemary sprigs**
4 **garlic cloves**
¼ **cup freshly grated Parmesan cheese**

Toppings: shaved Parmesan cheese, sliced fresh chives, freshly ground black pepper

1. Preheat the oven to 425°F. Remove discolored leaves from the Brussels sprouts. Remove and discard stem ends, and cut the sprouts into quarters. Toss with the olive oil, kosher salt, and ½ teaspoon freshly ground black pepper, and place in a single layer on a baking sheet. Bake at 425°F for 25 minutes or until golden and tender, stirring halfway through.

2. Meanwhile, stir together the cream, rosemary, and garlic in a medium saucepan. Cook over medium, stirring occasionally, 15 to 20 minutes or until reduced to about 1 cup. Discard the rosemary and garlic. Stir in the grated Parmesan cheese. Drizzle over the Brussels sprouts mixture. Top with the shaved Parmesan cheese, sliced chives, and black pepper, and serve immediately.

SHREDDED BRUSSELS SPROUTS SALAD

Raw, shredded Brussels sprouts make a crisp, crunchy base for a salad. Add a few simple toppings and homemade vinaigrette, and you have a refreshing holiday side.

SERVES 12 · **HANDS-ON:** 22 minutes · **TOTAL:** 22 minutes

12 **very thin pancetta slices**
¼ **cup olive oil**
1 **tablespoon stone-ground Dijon mustard**
¼ **teaspoon table salt**
¼ **teaspoon freshly ground black pepper**

¼ **teaspoon firmly packed lemon zest**
2 **tablespoons fresh lemon juice**
1 **garlic clove, minced**
2 **pounds baby Brussels sprouts, thinly sliced**

½ **cup chopped walnuts, toasted**
2 **ounces fresh Parmesan cheese, shaved**

1. Cook the pancetta in a large nonstick skillet over medium 5 minutes or until crisp, turning occasionally. Drain on paper towels.

2. Whisk together the olive oil and next 6 ingredients in a large bowl. Add the Brussels sprouts and walnuts; toss to coat. Divide the salad among 12 plates. Top each salad with 1 pancetta crisp, and sprinkle with cheese.

ROASTED ASPARAGUS WITH HOT BACON DRESSING

This dressing has the perfect balance of smoky, sweet, and salty flavors.

SERVES 10 · **HANDS-ON:** 5 minutes · **TOTAL:** 30 minutes

3 pounds fresh asparagus
2 tablespoons olive oil
1 teaspoon table salt
¾ teaspoon freshly ground black pepper

8 hickory-smoked bacon slices
1 shallot, minced
2 large garlic cloves, minced
⅓ cup white wine vinegar

2 tablespoons honey
1 teaspoon Dijon mustard

1. Preheat the oven to 450°F. Snap off and discard tough ends of the asparagus. Place the asparagus on a large baking sheet. Drizzle with the oil; sprinkle with ¾ teaspoon of the salt and ½ teaspoon of the pepper, tossing to coat.

2. Bake at 450°F for 20 to 25 minutes or just until crisp-tender. Place the asparagus on a serving platter; keep warm.

3. While the asparagus bakes, cook the bacon in a large skillet over medium-high until crisp; remove the bacon, reserving ¼ cup of the drippings in skillet. Crumble the bacon, and set aside.

4. Sauté the shallot and garlic in hot drippings 2 minutes or just until tender. Whisk in the vinegar, honey, mustard, remaining ¼ teaspoon salt, and remaining ¼ teaspoon pepper. Cook 1 minute or until thoroughly heated. Remove from heat; stir in the crumbled bacon. Drizzle the hot dressing over the asparagus. Serve immediately.

BROWN RICE-QUINOA PILAF WITH NUTS AND DRIED FRUIT

This simple, flavorful side dish uses prepared rice to save time in the kitchen during the holidays.

SERVES 8 · **HANDS-ON:** 14 minutes · **TOTAL:** 14 minutes

¼ cup chopped fresh parsley
3 tablespoons lemon juice
½ teaspoon table salt
½ teaspoon freshly ground black pepper

5 tablespoons olive oil
1 large shallot, minced
1 garlic clove, minced
¾ cup chopped walnuts, toasted

¾ cup chopped dried apricots
⅓ cup currants
4 (8.5-ounce) packages ready-to-heat quinoa-and-brown rice pilaf with garlic

1. Combine the first 4 ingredients and 3 tablespoons of the olive oil.

2. Sauté the shallot and garlic in remaining 2 tablespoons olive oil in a large skillet over medium-high 3 minutes or until tender and beginning to brown. Stir in the walnuts, next 3 ingredients, and lemon juice mixture. Cook, stirring constantly, 2 minutes or until thoroughly heated.

NOTE: We tested with Seeds of Change Quinoa & Brown Rice.

ROOT VEGETABLE GRATIN

Use a mandoline to cut vegetables into thin, uniform slices.

SERVES 8 to 10 · **HANDS-ON:** 27 minutes · **TOTAL:** 1 hour, 52 minutes

Vegetable cooking spray
3 cups heavy cream
6 garlic cloves, smashed
1 pound carrots, peeled and diagonally sliced
4 teaspoons chopped fresh thyme

1 teaspoon table salt
1 teaspoon freshly ground black pepper
6 ounces Gruyère cheese, shredded
1 pound parsnips, peeled and diagonally sliced

¾ pound turnips, peeled and thinly sliced
¾ pound rutabaga, peeled and thinly sliced
1 cup panko (Japanese-style breadcrumbs)
2 tablespoons butter, melted

1. Preheat the oven to 400°F. Grease a 13- x 9-inch baking dish with cooking spray. Combine cream and garlic in a saucepan. Cook, stirring, over medium 5 minutes or just until mixture simmers (do not boil). Remove and let stand 15 minutes. Remove and discard garlic. Cover and keep warm.
2. Arrange the carrots in an even layer in the prepared baking dish. Sprinkle with ¾ teaspoon of the thyme, ¼ teaspoon of the salt, ¼ teaspoon of the pepper, and ⅓ cup of the cheese. Repeat layers 3 times, 1 time with each remaining vegetable, plus equal amounts of the herbs and seasonings. (Sprinkle ⅓ cup of the cheese over each of the first 2 repeated layers. Do not sprinkle cheese on the third repeated layer.) Pour the cream over the vegetables.
3. Bake, covered, at 400°F for 30 minutes or until vegetables are tender. Press down top layer using a metal spatula. Uncover and bake at 400°F for 35 minutes or until the cream is thickened.
4. Combine the panko, butter, remaining ½ cup cheese, and remaining 1 teaspoon thyme; sprinkle over top of casserole. Uncover and bake at 400°F for 10 more minutes or until top is golden brown. Let stand 10 minutes before serving.

Roasted Asparagus with Hot Bacon Dressing

Root Vegetable Gratin

Brown Rice-Quinoa Pilaf with Nuts and Dried Fruit

DIRTY RICE RISOTTO

*Adding hot broth slowly to the mixture helps release the starch
from the rice, giving the risotto its characteristic creamy texture.*

SERVES 6 to 8 • **HANDS-ON:** 1 hour, 20 minutes • **TOTAL:** 1 hour, 20 minutes

5¼ cups chicken broth
8 ounces chicken livers
2 tablespoons olive oil
1 pound ground pork
1 medium-size yellow onion, finely chopped (about 1 cup)
3 celery ribs, finely chopped (about 1 cup)

1 green bell pepper, finely chopped
2 ounces (4 tablespoons) butter
3 garlic cloves, minced
1 cup Arborio rice
½ cup dry white wine
2½ teaspoons Creole seasoning

2 scallions, thinly sliced
¼ cup chopped fresh flat-leaf parsley
1½ tablespoons fresh lemon juice
Garnish: large celery slices

1. Bring 5 cups of the chicken broth to a simmer in a large saucepan over medium-high. Maintain at a low simmer until ready to use.

2. Meanwhile, sauté the livers in hot oil in a Dutch oven over medium 5 minutes or until cooked. Remove the cooked livers, and finely chop. Add the ground pork to Dutch oven, and cook, stirring occasionally, 10 minutes or until deep golden brown. Remove from Dutch oven using a slotted spoon, and drain on paper towels. Stir the ground pork into the chopped liver mixture.

3. Add the onion, celery, bell pepper, and 1 tablespoon of the butter to Dutch oven, and sauté 10 minutes or until tender. Stir in the minced garlic, and sauté 1 minute.

4. Add 1 tablespoon of the butter to Dutch oven, and stir until melted. Add the rice, and cook, stirring constantly, 1 minute or until fragrant.

5. Stir in the white wine, and cook, stirring often, 2 minutes or until nearly dry. Add 1 cup of the hot chicken broth, and cook, stirring constantly, until the liquid is absorbed. Repeat with the remaining hot chicken broth, 1 cup at a time, until the liquid is absorbed. (Total cooking time is 20 to 25 minutes.) Remove from heat.

6. Stir in the liver-and-pork mixture, Creole seasoning, next 3 ingredients, and remaining 2 tablespoons butter. Stir in remaining ¼ cup broth, if desired. Serve immediately.

BROCCOLINI WITH PECANS AND CANE SYRUP VINAIGRETTE

Easy, in-a-pinch substitutions: Use molasses for cane syrup and broccoli florets in place of fresh broccolini. Pomegranate seeds add a festive touch.

SERVES 6 to 8 • **HANDS-ON:** 10 minutes • **TOTAL:** 25 minutes, including vinaigrette

CANE SYRUP VINAIGRETTE:
- ⅔ cup olive oil
- ⅓ cup apple cider vinegar
- 2½ tablespoons pure cane syrup
- 1 tablespoon Creole mustard
- ¼ teaspoon kosher salt
- ¼ teaspoon freshly ground black pepper
- ⅛ teaspoon ground red pepper

BROCCOLINI WITH PECANS:
- 8 quarts water
- ¼ cup kosher salt
- 3 bunches fresh broccolini (about ½ pound), trimmed
- 1 cup toasted chopped pecans
- Garnish: pomegranate seeds

1. Make the broccolini: Bring the 8 quarts water and salt to a boil in a large stockpot over high. Gently stir in the broccolini, and cook 3 to 4 minutes or until tender. Drain and transfer to a large bowl.

2. Make the vinaigrette: Whisk together the olive oil and next 6 ingredients in a medium bowl.

3. Toss together the broccolini and 2 tablespoons of the vinaigrette. Top with the toasted chopped pecans, and serve immediately with remaining vinaigrette.

CRANBERRY-HORSERADISH CHUTNEY

This ruby-red chutney is a spectacular blend of sweet, tart, and savory flavors that will enhance your holiday meal.

MAKES 1¾ cups · **HANDS-ON:** 17 minutes · **TOTAL:** 2 hours, 31 minutes

½ **vanilla bean, split**
⅔ **cup sugar**
½ **cup ruby port**

1 **(12-ounce) package fresh cranberries**

¼ **cup prepared horseradish**

1. Scrape the seeds from the vanilla bean. Combine the vanilla bean seeds, bean pod, sugar, port, and cranberries in a medium saucepan. Bring to a boil; reduce heat, and simmer 10 minutes or until cranberry skins begin to split and liquid thickens. Remove from heat.
2. Remove and discard vanilla bean pod. Stir horseradish into mixture. Cover and chill 2 hours.

CRANBERRY ROASTED WINTER VEGETABLES

Sweet-tart cranberries up the flavor ante of traditional roasted veggies.

SERVES 8 · **HANDS-ON:** 30 minutes · **TOTAL:** 1 hour, 5 minutes

Vegetable cooking spray
4 **large carrots (about 1½ pounds), halved lengthwise and cut into 1-inch pieces**
3 **large turnips (about 2 pounds), peeled and cut into 1-inch pieces***

1 **pound Brussels sprouts, halved (quartered, if large)**
1 **tablespoon minced fresh rosemary**
2 **teaspoons olive oil**
¾ **teaspoon table salt**

¼ **teaspoon freshly ground black pepper**
1 **cup fresh or thawed frozen cranberries**
4 **teaspoons molasses**

1. Preheat the oven to 400°F. Lightly grease 2 large jelly-roll pans with cooking spray; place carrots and turnips in 1 pan and Brussels sprouts in the second pan. Divide the rosemary and next 3 ingredients between the two pans; toss each to coat.
2. Bake both pans at 400°F at the same time. Bake the carrot mixture at 400°F for 30 minutes, stirring once; add the cranberries, and bake for 5 more minutes or until carrots and turnips are tender and browned and cranberry skins begin to split. Bake the Brussels sprouts at 400°F for 15 to 20 minutes or until tender and browned, stirring once.
3. Remove the vegetables from the oven, and combine in a large serving bowl. Drizzle with the molasses, and toss to coat.

* 2 pounds parsnips may be substituted.

Cranberry-Horseradish Chutney

CREAMED ONION TART

Old-school creamed onions get an inventive update in this savory tart. Serve as a side dish or pair a wedge with a salad for a light meal any time of day.

SERVES 8 · **HANDS-ON:** 45 minutes · **TOTAL:** 1 hour, 55 minutes

½ (14.1-ounce) package refrigerated piecrusts

Vegetable cooking spray

3 thick bacon slices, cut into ½-inch pieces

1 tablespoon butter

2 pounds onions, thinly sliced

Pinch of table salt

½ cup crème fraîche

1 tablespoon chopped fresh sage

1 tablespoon chopped fresh thyme

1 teaspoon kosher salt

¾ teaspoon ground black pepper

½ teaspoon freshly grated nutmeg

3 large eggs, lightly beaten

1. Preheat the oven to 400°F. Fit piecrust into a 9-inch tart pan lightly coated with cooking spray. Bake the crust at 400°F for 8 to 10 minutes or until lightly browned. Cool.

2. Cook the bacon in a large skillet over medium-high, stirring occasionally until crisp; remove bacon, and drain on paper towels. Reserve the drippings in the skillet.

3. Reduce the heat to medium, and melt the butter with the drippings; add the onions and a pinch of salt. Cook, stirring often, 5 minutes. Cover and cook about 10 more minutes or until onions are soft and lightly browned. Uncover and cook, stirring often, 2 to 3 minutes or until liquid evaporates. Remove the skillet from heat, and cool completely.

4. Whisk together the crème fraîche and next 6 ingredients in a medium bowl. Stir in the bacon and onions. Spread the mixture in the prepared crust.

5. Bake at 400°F for 25 minutes or until golden. Cool on a wire rack 10 minutes before slicing.

BROWN BUTTER GREEN BEANS WITH LEMON PEPPER ALMONDS

Green beans are a favorite staple at the holiday table. These get a boost of flavor and lemony crunch from crispy almonds that can also double as a snack.

SERVES 12 · **HANDS-ON:** 10 minutes · **TOTAL:** 1 hour, 11 minutes

Parchment paper
1 large egg white
1 tablespoon water
½ pound sliced almonds
1 tablespoon sugar
1 teaspoon kosher salt
1 teaspoon ground coriander

1 teaspoon freshly ground black pepper
½ teaspoon lemon zest
1½ pounds haricots verts (French green beans), trimmed
6 ounces (¾ cup) butter

3 tablespoons fresh lemon juice
¼ teaspoon table salt
¼ teaspoon freshly ground black pepper

1. Preheat the oven to 275°F. Line a large rimmed baking sheet with parchment paper. Whisk together the egg white and 1 tablespoon water in a large bowl until frothy. Add the almonds, tossing to coat.

2. Combine the sugar and next 4 ingredients in a large zip-top plastic freezer bag. Remove the almonds from the egg white mixture using a slotted spoon; place in the bag. Seal the bag, and shake until the almonds are coated. Spread the nuts in a single layer on the prepared baking sheet.

3. Bake at 275°F for 15 minutes. Toss gently, and bake at 275°F for 14 more minutes. Cool completely on pan on a wire rack (about 30 minutes). (Almonds will become crisp as they cool.)

4. Cook the green beans in boiling water to cover 6 minutes; drain. Plunge the beans into ice water to stop the cooking process. Drain and pat dry with paper towels.

5. Melt the butter in a large skillet over medium heat. Cook 3 minutes or until butter begins to turn golden brown. Add the beans, lemon juice, and next 2 ingredients. Cook 5 minutes or until the beans are thoroughly heated, stirring often. Transfer the beans to a large serving platter; sprinkle with desired amount of almonds. Serve immediately. Cover and store any remaining almonds in an airtight container up to 1 week.

Roasted Garlic Duchess Potatoes

ROASTED GARLIC DUCHESS POTATOES

Want to make a fancy presentation and don't have a pastry bag? A 1-gallon zip-top plastic freezer bag will do the trick. Simply snip a small hole in one corner of the bag, and pipe.

SERVES 8 to 10 • **HANDS-ON:** 30 minutes • **TOTAL:** 2 hours

Parchment paper
1 garlic bulb
2 tablespoons olive oil

3 tablespoons plus ¼ teaspoon kosher salt
3 pounds russet potatoes, peeled and cubed

5 tablespoons (⅓ cup) butter
¼ cup heavy cream
2 large egg yolks

1. Preheat the oven to 425°F. Line 2 baking sheets with parchment paper. Cut off pointed end of the garlic bulb; place bulb on a piece of aluminum foil. Drizzle with the oil, and sprinkle with ¼ teaspoon of the kosher salt. Fold foil to seal. Bake at 425°F for 30 minutes; cool 15 minutes. Squeeze the pulp from garlic cloves into a small bowl, and mash with a spoon until smooth.
2. Place the potatoes and remaining 3 tablespoons salt in a large saucepan with cold water to cover by 2 inches. Bring to a boil over medium; boil 25 minutes or until potatoes are tender. Drain and return to pan. Reduce heat to medium-low. Cook, gently stirring often, 5 minutes or until dry. Remove from heat.
3. Simmer the butter and cream in a small saucepan over medium. (Do not boil.) Remove from heat.
4. Transfer the potatoes to a large bowl; mash with a potato ricer or masher until free of lumps. Stir in the hot cream mixture, egg yolks, and roasted garlic, until thoroughly combined. Spoon the potato mixture into a pastry bag fitted with a star tip. Pipe 3-inch-wide mounds 2 inches apart on the prepared baking sheets.
5. Bake at 425°F for 20 to 25 minutes or until tops are lightly browned. Serve immediately.

POTATOES PATIO

A combo of cheeses makes these luxurious baked potatoes all the more delicious.

SERVES 10 to 12 • **HANDS-ON:** 25 minutes • **TOTAL:** 1 hour, 40 minutes

Butter
2 cups heavy cream
1¾ teaspoons table salt
1 garlic clove, pressed
¾ teaspoon freshly ground black pepper

¼ teaspoon ground nutmeg
3 pounds russet potatoes, peeled and thinly sliced
2 cups freshly grated Gruyère cheese

2 tablespoons freshly grated Parmesan cheese

1. Preheat the oven to 350°F. Grease a 13- x 9-inch baking dish with butter. Stir together the cream and next 4 ingredients in a medium bowl. Let stand 5 minutes.
2. Arrange a single layer of potatoes in the baking dish. Pour ¼ cup of the cream mixture over potatoes; sprinkle with ¼ cup of the Gruyère cheese. Repeat layers 7 more times. Top with the Parmesan.
3. Bake, covered with foil, at 350°F for 45 minutes. Uncover and bake for 15 to 20 more minutes or until golden brown and potatoes are tender. Cool on a wire rack 10 minutes.

TWO-POTATO GRATIN

"This luscious gratin strikes a happy middle chord for those hungry for potatoes and those vying for a sweet potato casserole." —Nancy Vienneau, author of Third Thursday Community Potluck Cookbook, *from which this recipe was adapted.*

SERVES 10 to 12 · **HANDS-ON:** 45 minutes · **TOTAL:** 1 hour, 45 minutes

---

Butter
2   shallots, diced
2   ounces (¼ cup) butter
2   cups heavy cream
2   tablespoons chopped parsley
1   tablespoon chopped chives

1   teaspoon kosher salt
½   teaspoon ground white pepper
⅛   teaspoon freshly grated nutmeg
1½   pounds Yukon Gold potatoes
1½   pounds sweet potatoes

2   cups milk
1½   cups (6 ounces) shredded Gruyère cheese
¼   cup (1 ounce) grated Parmesan cheese

1. Preheat the oven to 375°F. Grease a 13- x 9-inch baking dish with butter. Sauté the shallots in 3 tablespoons of the butter in a saucepan over medium 2 minutes. Stir in the cream and next 5 ingredients; cook 2 minutes. Remove from heat; cool 15 minutes.

2. Meanwhile, peel and thinly slice all the potatoes. Combine the sliced potatoes and milk in a large microwave-safe bowl. Cover with plastic wrap, and microwave at HIGH 5 minutes. Uncover and gently stir mixture. Re-cover and microwave 5 more minutes. Drain the mixture, discarding milk.

3. Layer one-third of the Yukon Gold potatoes in the prepared baking dish; top with one-third of the sweet potatoes. Spoon one-third of the cream mixture over the potatoes, and sprinkle with ½ cup of the Gruyère cheese. Repeat layers twice, and top with the Parmesan cheese. Cut remaining 1 tablespoon butter into small pieces, and dot over the top. Cover with foil.

4. Bake at 375°F for 30 minutes. Uncover; bake at 375°F for 20 more minutes or until browned. Let stand 10 minutes.

HERBED POTATO PANCAKES WITH CHIVE CRÈME FRAÎCHE

These potato cakes are delicious alongside a standing rib or pork roast on the holiday table.

SERVES 14 · **HANDS-ON:** 25 minutes · **TOTAL:** 25 minutes

2½ pounds russet potatoes
¼ cup (1.1 ounces) flour
¼ cup chopped scallions
¼ cup chopped fresh parsley
½ teaspoon table salt

2 large eggs, lightly beaten
¾ teaspoon freshly ground black pepper, divided
½ cup canola oil

1 (8-ounce) container crème fraîche
½ teaspoon packed lemon zest
1 tablespoon chopped fresh chives

1. Preheat the oven to 200°F. Line a large baking sheet with aluminum foil.
2. Peel and shred the potatoes. Place in batches, in a clean dish towel. Holding towel over a bowl, squeeze the potatoes dry, and place in a large bowl to measure 7 cups. Reserve liquid and white potato starch. Slowly pour off and discard liquid, leaving white potato starch in bottom to measure about 1½ tablespoons. Add starch, flour, next 4 ingredients, and ½ teaspoon pepper to potatoes.
3. Heat 2 tablespoons of the oil in a 12-inch skillet over medium-high. Shape potato mixture by about ¼ cupfuls into 28 (¼-inch-thick) cakes. Fry 4 cakes in hot oil 2 minutes on each side or until edges are crisp; drain. Transfer the cakes to prepared baking sheet; keep warm in 200°F oven. Repeat procedure 6 times with remaining oil and potato cakes.
4. Stir together the crème fraîche, next 2 ingredients, and remaining ¼ teaspoon pepper in a small bowl. Serve with the potato cakes.

SWEET POTATO PONE

The sweet-and-savory flavors in this favorite holiday bread complement smoked ham perfectly.

SERVES 12 to 15 · **HANDS-ON:** 15 minutes · **TOTAL:** 55 minutes

3 pounds sweet potatoes
3 ounces (6 tablespoons) unsalted butter, softened
1 cup firmly packed light brown sugar

3 large eggs
6 tablespoons bourbon
¾ teaspoon freshly ground black pepper
1½ teaspoons table salt

3 ounces (6 tablespoons) butter, melted
⅜ teaspoon ground red pepper
1½ cups pecan pieces

1. Preheat the oven to 375°F. Peel and coarsely grate the sweet potatoes to measure 8 packed cups.
2. Beat the softened butter and ¾ cup of the brown sugar at medium speed with an electric mixer until fluffy. Add the eggs, 1 at a time, beating well. Stir in the bourbon, black pepper, and 1¼ teaspoons of the salt. Stir in the sweet potato.
3. Cook 3 tablespoons melted butter in a 12-inch cast-iron skillet over medium-high until lightly browned. Add the potato mixture, spreading to edges of skillet. Increase heat to high, and cook, uncovered, 1 minute or until steam begins to escape. Bake, uncovered, at 375°F for 20 minutes.
4. Combine the ground red pepper, remaining ¼ cup brown sugar, remaining 3 tablespoons melted butter, and remaining ¼ teaspoon salt in a medium bowl. Add the pecans, tossing to coat.
5. Sprinkle the pecan mixture over potato mixture, and bake, uncovered, 20 more minutes or until pecans are lightly browned.

CARAMELIZED ONION-SAUSAGE CRACKER STUFFING

*Unlike traditional stuffing or dressing, this recipe uses
store-bought crackers as its base to create a crisp, crunchy crust.*

SERVES 6 to 8 • **HANDS-ON:** 37 minutes • **TOTAL:** 1 hour, 42 minutes

Vegetable cooking spray
1½ (1-pound) packages
    whole-wheat round buttery
    crackers, coarsely crushed
1 pound ground pork sausage
2 tablespoons olive oil
8 cups vertically sliced sweet
    onions (about 5 onions)

1 teaspoon sugar
1 cup chopped celery
    (about 4 ribs)
2 teaspoons chopped
    fresh sage
½ teaspoon table salt
½ teaspoon ground
    black pepper

5 garlic cloves, minced
2 large eggs
1½ cups chicken broth
3 ounces (6 tablespoons)
    butter, melted

1. Preheat the oven to 350°F. Lightly grease a 13- x 9-inch baking dish with cooking spray. Place the crushed crackers in a large bowl.

2. Cook the sausage in a large skillet over medium-high, stirring often, 7 minutes or until the meat crumbles and is no longer pink. Remove the sausage from the skillet using a slotted spoon, and add to the crushed crackers. Pour off the drippings, reserving 1 tablespoon drippings in skillet.

3. Add the olive oil to the drippings in the skillet. Add the onions and sugar; reduce heat to medium, and cook, stirring often, 20 minutes or until onions are caramel colored and very tender. Stir in the celery and next 4 ingredients; sauté 3 minutes or just until tender. Stir the onion mixture into sausage mixture.

4. Whisk the eggs in a bowl; whisk in the chicken broth. Pour the broth mixture over the cracker mixture, stirring until moistened. Spoon the mixture into the prepared baking dish; drizzle with the melted butter.

5. Bake, uncovered, at 350°F for 55 minutes or until the top is crisp. Let stand 10 minutes before serving.

CHEESE CRACKER-TOPPED SQUASH CASSEROLE

"We have a hard time getting our grandson to eat a vegetable. He loves goldfish crackers, so I came up with this recipe," says Southern Living reader Gerri Ellis. To copy the presentation pictured below, crush a few crackers and toss the crumbs with paprika. The whole fish will really stand out!

SERVES 8 to 10 · **HANDS-ON:** 20 minutes · **TOTAL:** 1 hour, 40 minutes

Butter
3 pounds yellow squash, chopped
2 pounds zucchini, chopped
1 medium onion, chopped
2 tablespoons kosher salt
½ cup sour cream

½ cup mayonnaise
1 large egg
1 (8-ounce) block extra-sharp Cheddar cheese, grated
½ teaspoon ground black pepper

2 cups fish-shaped Cheddar cheese crackers
2 tablespoons butter, melted

1. Preheat the oven to 350°F. Grease a 13- x 9-inch baking dish with butter. Place the squash and next 2 ingredients in a Dutch oven; add hot water 2 inches above squash-and-onion mixture. Add the salt to Dutch oven, and stir to dissolve. Bring the mixture to a boil over medium-high. Boil 10 minutes or until the squash is very tender when pierced with a fork. Drain the vegetable mixture well; let stand at room temperature 15 minutes to cool slightly.

2. Meanwhile, stir together the sour cream and mayonnaise in a large bowl. Lightly beat the egg, and stir into mayonnaise mixture. Gently stir in the cheese, pepper, and cooked squash mixture; spoon mixture into the prepared baking dish.

3. Bake at 350°F for 40 minutes or until bubbly. Combine the cheese crackers and melted butter, and toss to coat. Arrange over the casserole. Bake at 350°F for 10 more minutes. Remove from the oven, and let stand 5 minutes before serving.

CORN PUDDING WITH LEEKS AND THYME

Add leeks and thyme to this traditional standby and you'll not only enhance the sweetness of the corn, but you'll also create a new family favorite for your holiday table.

SERVES 12 to 15 · HANDS-ON: 26 minutes · TOTAL: 1 hour, 16 minutes

Vegetable cooking spray
8 ears fresh corn, husks removed
3 small leeks
4 applewood-smoked bacon slices
1 large sweet onion, chopped (1 cup)
¼ cup (1.1 ounces) all-purpose flour
1 cup heavy cream
¾ cup half-and-half
2 teaspoons chopped fresh thyme leaves
2 teaspoons chopped fresh parsley
½ teaspoon table salt
¼ teaspoon freshly ground black pepper
4 large eggs, beaten
1 (8-ounce) package shredded Monterey Jack cheese

1. Preheat the oven to 375°F. Lightly grease a 13- x 9-inch baking dish with cooking spray. Cut the tips of corn kernels from the cobs into a large bowl; scrape milk and remaining pulp from cobs. Remove and discard root ends and dark green tops of the leeks. Cut the leeks in half lengthwise, and rinse thoroughly under cold running water to remove grit and sand. Coarsely chop the leeks.

2. Cook the bacon in a large skillet over medium until crisp; drain, reserving drippings in skillet. Sauté the leeks and onion in hot drippings over medium-high 6 minutes or until tender. Sprinkle the flour over onion mixture; cook, stirring constantly, 1 minute. Whisk in the cream and half-and-half; cook, stirring constantly, 2 to 3 minutes or until thickened. Remove from heat. Cool slightly.

3. Stir the thyme and next 4 ingredients into the corn. Stir in the onion mixture and cheese. Pour the corn mixture into the prepared baking dish. Bake at 375°F for 45 minutes or until set and golden. Let stand 5 minutes before serving.

FEATHERLIGHT DINNER ROLLS

Try your hand at homemade rolls this year instead of purchasing those in the freezer section. A heavy-duty stand mixer makes quick work of these delicate rolls.

MAKES 1 dozen · **HANDS-ON:** 17 minutes · **TOTAL:** 2 hours, 17 minutes

1 cup warm milk (100° to 110°F)
1 (¼-ounce) envelope active dry yeast
1 teaspoon sugar
3 cups (13.5 ounces) all-purpose flour
2 tablespoons sugar
1 teaspoon table salt
5 tablespoons (⅓ cup) melted butter
1 large egg, lightly beaten
Vegetable cooking spray

1. Stir together the first 3 ingredients in a 2-cup glass measuring cup; let stand 5 minutes.

2. Combine the flour and next 2 ingredients in the bowl of a heavy-duty electric stand mixer. Add 3 tablespoons of the melted butter, egg, and yeast mixture; beat at low speed, using dough hook attachment, 3 minutes or until blended and a soft dough forms. Increase speed to medium-low, and beat 4 minutes or until the dough is smooth and elastic but still slightly sticky. Cover bowl of dough with plastic wrap, and let rise in a warm place (80° to 85°F), free from drafts, 1 hour or until doubled in bulk.

3. Lightly grease a 13- x 9-inch pan with cooking spray. Punch the dough down. Turn the dough out onto a lightly floured surface. Divide the dough into 12 equal portions. Gently shape each portion into a 2-inch ball; place in the prepared pan. Brush the tops with 1 tablespoon of the melted butter. Cover and let rise in a warm place (80° to 85°F), free from drafts, 45 minutes or until doubled in bulk.

4. Preheat the oven to 375°F. Bake the rolls at 375°F for 15 minutes or until golden brown. Transfer the rolls from the pan to a wire rack, and brush with remaining 1 tablespoon melted butter. Serve warm, or cool completely (about 30 minutes).

Sweet Potato Tartlets with Crème Fraîche Topping, page 146
Coconut-Citrus Pavlova, page 147

Triple Chocolate Brownie-Mousse Stacks, page 144

Gingerbread Baked Alaska, page 157

Raspberry Swirl Icebox Pie, page 139

DECADENT DESSERTS

Because no holiday meal is complete without a sweet grand finale, here are swoon-worthy options for all tastes.

PRALINE CREAM BEIGNET TOWER

Make the praline filling and dough up to two days ahead.

SERVES 12 to 15 · **HANDS-ON:** 2 hours · **TOTAL:** 6 hours, 35 minutes

PRALINE CREAM FILLING:
- ¾ cup firmly packed light brown sugar
- ¼ cup cornstarch
- ¼ teaspoon table salt
- 2½ cups half-and-half
- 4 large egg yolks
- 3 tablespoons butter
- 1 tablespoon pecan liqueur

BEIGNETS:
- 1 (¼-ounce) envelope active dry yeast
- 1½ cups warm water (100° to 110°F)
- ½ cup plus 1 teaspoon granulated sugar
- 1 cup evaporated milk
- 2 large eggs, lightly beaten
- 1 teaspoon table salt
- ¼ cup shortening

- 6½ to 7 cups bread flour
- Vegetable cooking spray
- Vegetable oil
- 120 heavy-duty 2-inch wooden picks
- 1 (17⅞- x 4¹⁵⁄₁₆-inch) plastic foam cone
- Powdered sugar

1. Make the filling: Whisk together the first 3 ingredients in a large heavy saucepan; whisk together half-and-half and egg yolks in a medium bowl. Gradually whisk the half-and-half mixture into the brown sugar mixture, and cook over medium, whisking constantly, about 7 minutes or until the mixture just begins to bubble. Cook, whisking constantly, 1 more minute; remove from heat, and whisk in the butter and pecan liqueur. Whisk until the butter melts. Spoon the mixture into a medium bowl, and place plastic wrap directly onto the filling (to prevent a film from forming). Cool 30 minutes. Chill 4 hours to 2 days.

2. Meanwhile, make the beignets: Combine the yeast, ½ cup of the warm water (100° to 110°F), and 1 teaspoon of the granulated sugar in bowl of a heavy-duty stand mixer; let stand 5 minutes. Add the evaporated milk, eggs, salt, and remaining ½ cup granulated sugar to yeast mixture, beating at medium speed until combined.

3. Microwave remaining 1 cup warm water in a 2-cup glass measuring cup until hot (about 115°F); stir in shortening until melted. Add to the yeast mixture. Beat at low speed, gradually adding 4 cups of the flour, until smooth. Gradually add remaining 2½ to 3 cups flour, beating until a sticky dough forms. Transfer to a bowl lightly greased with cooking spray; lightly grease top of dough with cooking spray. Cover and chill 4 hours to 2 days.

4. Turn the dough out onto a heavily floured surface; roll half of dough to ¼-inch thickness. (Refrigerate remaining dough until ready to use.) Cut into 2-inch squares with a pizza wheel or a sharp knife. Repeat with remaining half of dough.

5. Pour the oil to a depth of 2 to 3 inches into a large Dutch oven; heat to 360°F. Fry the dough squares, in batches, 1 to 2 minutes on each side or until golden brown. Drain on a wire rack.

6. Insert a small metal tip (we used a #17) into a large pastry bag. Using a long wooden skewer, poke a hole in the side of each beignet. Fill pastry bag with half of the chilled filling. Pipe a small amount into each beignet. Repeat with remaining filling and beignets.

7. Assemble the tower: Starting at bottom, insert 1 pick into the side of the cone. Press 1 beignet onto pick. Repeat with remaining picks and beignets, covering entire cone. Dust entire beignet-covered cone heavily with powdered sugar.

BELGIAN SPICE COOKIES

To create a lacy design on these cookies (also known as Speculoos), place a stencil or doily over the cooled cookies before dusting with powdered sugar.

MAKES about 2 dozen · **HANDS-ON:** 10 minutes · **TOTAL:** 5 hours

1   cup (4.5 ounces)
   all-purpose flour
¼   teaspoon baking powder
¼   teaspoon baking soda
¼   teaspoon table salt

3   teaspoons pumpkin pie spice
4   ounces (½ cup) butter,
   softened
¼   cup turbinado sugar

¼   cup firmly packed
   light brown sugar
Parchment paper
½   cup powdered sugar

1. Stir together the flour, next 3 ingredients, and 1 teaspoon of the pumpkin pie spice in a small bowl. Beat the butter and next 2 ingredients in a medium bowl at medium speed with an electric mixer 2 to 3 minutes or until combined. Stir in the flour mixture just until blended. Shape the dough into a 2-inch-thick log; wrap in plastic wrap, and chill 4 hours to 3 days.

2. Preheat the oven to 325°F. Line a baking sheet with parchment paper. Slice dough log into ¼-inch-thick rounds. Place the cookies about 1 inch apart on the prepared baking sheet.

3. Bake at 325°F for 10 to 14 minutes or until cookies are fragrant and dry. Cool completely on a wire rack (about 30 minutes).

4. Stir together the powdered sugar and remaining 2 teaspoons pumpkin pie spice. Sift the powdered sugar mixture over cookies.

STRAWBERRY-PEACH CHAMPAGNE

Turn your afternoon tea into a Champagne tea with this fruit-infused drink.
Use a good-quality Champagne or dry Prosecco for the best flavor.

SERVES 8 · **HANDS-ON:** 14 minutes · **TOTAL:** 2 hours, 29 minutes

½   cup granulated sugar
½   cup sliced fresh strawberries
2   teaspoons fresh lemon juice
2   ripe peaches, peeled and cut into 1-inch pieces

1   cup water
1   (750-milliliter) bottle Champagne or sparkling wine, chilled

Garnish: sliced strawberries

1. Combine the first 5 ingredients in a small saucepan. Bring to a boil; remove from heat, and let stand 15 minutes. Process peach mixture in a blender until smooth. Pour peach mixture through a fine wire-mesh strainer into a bowl; discard solids. Cover and chill at least 2 hours.

2. Combine 2 cups of the syrup and Champagne in a pitcher, reserving remaining syrup for another use. Pour the Champagne mixture into 8 Champagne flutes.

BROWN SUGAR-PECAN BUTTONS

These buttons are a cross between a traditional shortbread and a wedding cookie,
but the addition of brown sugar makes them a chewy, buttery treat.

MAKES 1½ dozen · **HANDS-ON:** 11 minutes · **TOTAL:** 59 minutes

Parchment paper
8   ounces (1 cup) butter, softened
⅓   cup firmly packed light brown sugar

3   tablespoons granulated sugar
2¼ cups (10.1 ounces) all-purpose flour

⅓   cup finely chopped toasted pecans
1   cup powdered sugar
2   tablespoons milk

1. Preheat the oven to 325°F. Line a baking sheet with parchment paper.

2. Beat the butter and sugars at medium speed with an electric mixer until fluffy. Gradually add the flour and pecans, stirring well. (Dough will be slightly crumbly.) Pat or roll dough to ½-inch thickness on a lightly floured surface; cut with a 1½-inch round or fluted round cutter. Place on the prepared baking sheet.

3. Bake at 325°F for 23 minutes or just until bottoms are lightly browned. Cool 5 minutes. Transfer the cookies to a wire rack, and cool completely (20 minutes).

4. Stir together the powdered sugar and milk in a small bowl until smooth. Drizzle the glaze onto tops of cookies.

SALTED CHOCOLATE BOURBON TRUFFLES

Change the flavor of these by substituting your favorite liqueur for the bourbon. Whiskey, brandy, or coffee liqueur would also work well.

MAKES 2½ dozen • **HANDS-ON:** 28 minutes • **TOTAL:** 4 hours, 28 minutes

12 ounces semisweet chocolate, chopped
3 tablespoons unsalted butter
1 teaspoon vanilla extract
⅓ cup heavy cream
3 tablespoons bourbon
⅛ teaspoon sea salt
Unsweetened cocoa
Powdered sugar
Chocolate wafer cookies, finely ground
Wax paper

1. Combine the first 3 ingredients in a large microwave-safe bowl. Heat the cream and bourbon in a small saucepan over medium 3 to 4 minutes or until mixture is hot but not boiling. Pour the cream mixture over the chocolate. Let stand 1 minute.

2. Stir the chocolate mixture until melted and smooth. (If mixture doesn't melt completely, microwave at HIGH 30 seconds.) Stir in the sea salt. Cover and chill 3 hours or until firm. (Mixture can be prepared and chilled up to 2 days ahead.)

3. Shape the mixture into 1-inch balls (about 2 teaspoons per ball). Roll in the cocoa, powdered sugar, or finely ground chocolate wafers, as desired. Place on wax paper-lined baking sheets. Chill 1 hour.

Strawberry-Peach Champagne, Brown Sugar-Pecan Buttons, and Salted Chocolate Bourbon Truffles

PEPPERMINT SWIRL HOT CHOCOLATE

*Red-and-white-swirled, peppermint-flavored whipped cream
crowns this creamy hot chocolate for a twist on the candy cane theme.*

SERVES 8 · **HANDS-ON:** 27 minutes · **TOTAL:** 27 minutes

2   cups milk
1   (12-ounce) can evaporated milk
3   cups heavy cream
1   (12-ounce) package semisweet chocolate morsels

1   (10-ounce) package bittersweet chocolate morsels
½   teaspoon vanilla extract
Pinch of table salt
1   tablespoon powdered sugar

½   teaspoon peppermint extract
10 drops of red gel paste food coloring
Candy sprinkles

1. Whisk together the milks and 2 cups of the cream in a large saucepan. Cook, stirring constantly, over medium 15 minutes or until mixture comes to a boil. Reduce heat to low; whisk in the chocolate morsels, vanilla, and salt until chocolate is melted and smooth. Keep hot.

2. Beat remaining 1 cup cream until foamy; add powdered sugar and peppermint extract, beating until soft peaks form.

3. Pour the hot chocolate into 8 mugs. Insert a star-shaped tip into a large decorating bag; drop food coloring around inside of bag, allowing it to drip down sides. Carefully spoon whipped cream into bag. Pipe the whipped cream onto the hot chocolate in the mugs; top each serving with sprinkles. Serve immediately.

Peppermint Swirl Hot Chocolate

PEPPERMINT RED VELVET LAYER CHEESECAKE

This festive cake, pictured on the cover, marries two favorite holiday flavors: chocolate and peppermint.

SERVES 12 • **HANDS-ON:** 45 minutes • **TOTAL TIME:** 13 hours, 45 minutes

CHEESECAKE LAYERS:
- 2 (8-inch) round disposable aluminum foil cake pans
- 1 (12-ounce) package white chocolate morsels
- 5 (8-ounce) packages cream cheese, softened
- 1 cup granulated sugar
- 2 large eggs
- 2 teaspoons vanilla extract
- 1 teaspoon peppermint extract

RED VELVET LAYERS:
- 1 cup butter, softened
- 2½ cups granulated sugar
- 6 large eggs
- 3 cups all-purpose flour
- 3 tablespoons cocoa
- ¼ teaspoon baking soda
- 8 ounces sour cream
- 2 teaspoons vanilla extract
- 2 (1-ounce) bottles red liquid food coloring
- 3 (8-inch) round disposable aluminum foil cake pans

WHITE CHOCOLATE FROSTING:
- 2 (4-ounce) white chocolate baking bars, chopped
- ½ cup boiling water
- 1 cup butter, softened
- 1 (32-ounce) package powdered sugar, sifted
- ½ teaspoon peppermint extract
- ⅛ teaspoon table salt

RED AND WHITE CANDY CURLS
- 1 bag red candy melts
- 1 bag white candy melts

1. Make the Cheesecake Layers: Preheat oven to 300°F. Line bottom and sides of 2 disposable cake pans with aluminum foil, allowing 2 to 3 inches to extend over the sides; lightly grease foil.

2. Microwave the white chocolate morsels in a bowl according to package directions; cool 10 minutes.

3. Beat the cream cheese and melted chocolate at medium speed with an electric mixer until creamy; gradually add the sugar, beating well. Add the eggs, 1 at a time, beating just until the yellow disappears after each addition. Stir in the vanilla and peppermint extracts. Pour into prepared pans.

4. Bake at 300°F for 30 to 35 minutes or until almost set. Turn oven off. Let cheesecakes stand in oven, with door closed, 30 minutes. Remove from oven to wire racks; cool completely (about 1½ hours). Cover and chill 8 hours, or freeze 24 hours to 2 days.

5. Make the Red Velvet Layers: Preheat the oven to 350°F. Beat the butter at medium speed with a heavy-duty electric stand mixer until creamy. Gradually add the sugar, beating until light and fluffy. Add the eggs, 1 at a time, beating just until blended after each addition.

6. Stir together flour and next 2 ingredients; add to butter mixture alternately with sour cream, beginning and ending with flour mixture. Beat at low speed until blended after each addition. Stir in vanilla and food coloring. Spoon batter into 3 greased and floured 8-inch disposable cake pans.

7. Bake at 350°F for 20 to 24 minutes or until a wooden pick inserted in center comes out clean. Cool in pans on wire racks 10 minutes. Remove from pans to wire racks; cool completely (about 1 hour).

8. Make the Frosting: Whisk together the chocolate and ½ cup boiling water until chocolate melts. Cool 20 minutes; chill 30 minutes. Beat butter and chilled chocolate mixture at low speed until blended. Beat at medium speed 1 minute. Increase speed to high; beat 2 to 3 minutes or until fluffy. Gradually add the powdered sugar, peppermint, and salt, beating at low speed until blended. Increase speed to high; beat 1 to 2 minutes or until smooth and fluffy.

9. Assemble the Cake: Place 1 layer Red Velvet on a serving platter. Top with 1 Cheesecake layer. Repeat with the remaining layers of Red Velvet and Cheesecake, alternating and ending with Red Velvet on top. Spread the top and the sides of the cake with White Chocolate Frosting.

10. Make the Candy Curls: Place candy melts in separate bowls. Microwave in 30 second increments, stirring until melted. Spoon each color, alternating, into a mini loaf pan lined with plastic wrap. Using a knife, swirl together. Let stand until firm. Remove from pan. Drag a vegetable peeler across narrow side of candy block to form curls. Decorate top of cake with curls.

MOCHA PECAN PIE WITH IRISH WHIPPED CREAM

Rich flavors of chocolate and espresso intensify the ever-popular pecan pie.

SERVES 8 · **HANDS-ON:** 17 minutes · **TOTAL:** 7 hours, 52 minutes

1½ cups (6.75 ounces) all-purpose flour

4 ounces (½ cup) unsalted butter, cut up

2 teaspoons kosher salt

¼ cup ice water

1 cup sugar

2 tablespoons all-purpose flour

3 tablespoons unsweetened cocoa

2 teaspoons instant espresso granules

¼ teaspoon table salt

1 cup light corn syrup

3 tablespoons butter, melted

1 tablespoon heavy cream

2 teaspoons vanilla extract

3 large eggs, lightly beaten

1¼ cups chopped pecans

½ cup pecan halves

1 cup heavy cream

2 tablespoons Irish cream liqueur

⅛ teaspoon ground cinnamon

1. Preheat the oven to 350°F. Pulse the first 3 ingredients in a food processor 8 times or until mixture resembles coarse meal. Add the ice water, 1 tablespoon at a time, and pulse until a dough forms. Shape dough into a disk. Wrap dough in plastic wrap, and chill 1 hour. Roll the dough into a 13-inch circle on a floured surface. Fit into a 9-inch pie plate; fold edges under, and crimp. Chill 20 minutes.

2. Line the pastry with aluminum foil, and fill with pie weights or dried beans. Bake at 350°F for 15 minutes. Remove the weights and foil, and bake at 350°F for 10 minutes or until dry and set, but not brown. Cool completely on a wire rack (about 40 minutes).

3. Meanwhile, whisk together the sugar and next 4 ingredients in a medium bowl. Add the corn syrup and next 4 ingredients; whisk until blended. Stir in the chopped pecans. Pour the filling into the prepared crust. Carefully arrange the pecan halves around the edge of the filling.

4. Bake at 350°F for 1 hour and 10 minutes or until set, shielding edges with foil after 45 minutes to prevent excessive browning. Cool completely on a wire rack (about 4 hours).

5. Combine 1 cup cream, liqueur, and cinnamon in a bowl; beat at high speed with an electric mixer until soft peaks form. Cover and chill until ready to serve. Serve the pie topped with dollops of whipped cream. Sprinkle with extra cinnamon.

RASPBERRY SWIRL ICEBOX PIE

This colorful, make-ahead raspberry mousse pie in a pistachio-shortbread crust is perfect for no-fuss holiday entertaining.

SERVES 8 to 10 · **HANDS-ON:** 22 minutes · **TOTAL:** 7 hours, 8 minutes

½ cup pistachios
13 rectangular pure butter shortbread cookies, broken
2 ounces (¼ cup) butter, melted
Vegetable cooking spray

½ cup sugar
¼ cup water
1 envelope unflavored gelatin
2 tablespoons cold water
1 tablespoon fresh lemon juice

4 cups frozen raspberries, thawed
1 cup heavy cream
Garnishes: whipped cream, fresh raspberries, lemon zest, fresh mint sprigs

1. Preheat the oven to 350°F. Process the pistachios in a food processor until chopped. Add the cookies, and process until finely ground. Add the butter; pulse just until crumbs are moistened. Press the crumb mixture into the bottom and up the sides of a 9½-inch deep-dish pie plate lightly greased with cooking spray.

2. Bake at 350°F for 16 minutes or until golden brown. Cool completely on a wire rack (about 30 minutes).

3. Bring the sugar and ¼ cup water to a simmer in a small saucepan, stirring until sugar dissolves. Remove from heat.

4. Sprinkle the gelatin over 2 tablespoons cold water in a small bowl; let stand 1 minute. Add the gelatin mixture to warm sugar mixture, stirring until gelatin dissolves (about 2 minutes). Transfer to a large bowl; stir in the lemon juice.

5. Process the raspberries in clean food processor until smooth. Pour the raspberry puree through a wire-mesh strainer into a bowl, pressing with the back of a spoon to squeeze out juice. Discard the pulp and seeds. Whisk 1 cup raspberry puree into gelatin mixture, reserving remaining puree.

6. Beat the cream at medium speed with an electric mixer until soft peaks form. Whisk one-fourth of the whipped cream into gelatin mixture; fold in remaining whipped cream. Spoon the mixture into the prepared crust. Dollop remaining raspberry puree, by teaspoonfuls, onto top of pie; gently swirl into filling with a knife. Cover and chill for at least 6 hours or up to overnight.

NOTE: We tested with Walker's Pure Butter Shortbread.

EGGNOG CHEESECAKE WITH BOURBON CARAMEL

You can also use high-quality prepared caramel sauce. Warm it in a saucepan over low heat, then gradually stir in bourbon to taste.

SERVES 10 · **HANDS-ON:** 15 minutes · **TOTAL:** 11 hours, 36 minutes, including chill time

2 cups graham cracker crumbs (about 15 whole crackers)
4 ounces (½ cup) butter, melted
½ cup finely chopped pecans
2 tablespoons sugar
3 (8-ounce) packages cream cheese, softened

1¾ cups sugar
2 tablespoons all-purpose flour
½ teaspoon freshly grated nutmeg
4 large eggs
1 cup refrigerated eggnog
1 teaspoon vanilla extract

¼ cup light corn syrup
¼ cup water
¾ cup heavy cream
2 tablespoons bourbon
Sweetened whipped cream
Freshly grated nutmeg

1. Preheat the oven to 325°F. Stir together the first 4 ingredients in a medium bowl until well blended. Press the mixture on the bottom and 2 inches up the sides of a 9-inch springform pan. Bake at 325°F for 10 to 12 minutes or until lightly browned. Transfer to a wire rack, and cool completely (about 30 minutes).

2. Meanwhile, beat the cream cheese and 1 cup of the sugar at medium speed with a heavy-duty electric stand mixer until blended and smooth. Beat in the flour and nutmeg. Add the eggs, 1 at a time, beating just until blended after each addition. Add the eggnog and vanilla, beating until blended. Pour the batter into the prepared crust.

3. Bake at 325°F for 1 hour and 5 minutes or until almost set. Turn oven off. Let the cheesecake stand in the oven with the door closed 15 minutes. Remove the cheesecake from the oven, and gently run a knife around the outer edge of cheesecake to loosen from the sides of the pan. (Do not remove sides of pan.) Cool completely on a wire rack (about 1 hour). Cover and chill 8 to 24 hours.

4. Bring the corn syrup, ¼ cup water, and remaining ¾ cup sugar to a boil in a medium saucepan over medium-high. (Do not stir.) Boil, swirling occasionally after sugar begins to change color, 7 minutes or until dark amber. (Do not walk away from the pan because sugar will burn quickly once it begins to change color.) Remove from heat. Carefully whisk in ¾ cup cream (the mixture will bubble and spatter). Whisk constantly until bubbling stops. Whisk in the bourbon. Cover and chill until ready to use or up to 2 weeks.

5. Remove sides of pan from the cheesecake. Insert a medium-size metal star tip into a large decorating bag; fill with the whipped cream. Pipe the cream decoratively around the top edge of the cheesecake. Sprinkle with the freshly grated nutmeg. Heat the caramel until pourable. Drizzle each serving with caramel.

CHOCOLATE-PEPPERMINT CHEESECAKE

Don't worry if your cheesecake cracks; the light and fluffy layer of whipped cream will cover it.

SERVES 10 to 12 · **HANDS-ON:** 30 minutes · **TOTAL:** 11 hours, 50 minutes, including whipped cream

CRUST:
Vegetable cooking spray
2 cups chocolate wafer crumbs (about 35 wafers)
5 tablespoons (2.5 ounces) butter, melted
3 tablespoons sugar

FILLING:
1 cup semisweet chocolate morsels
¼ cup heavy cream
4 (8-ounce) packages cream cheese, softened
1 cup sugar
1 teaspoon vanilla extract
1 teaspoon peppermint extract
4 large eggs

WHIPPED PEPPERMINT CREAM:
2 cups heavy cream
¾ teaspoon peppermint extract
¾ cup powdered sugar
Garnish: crushed peppermint candies

1. Make the crust: Preheat the oven to 350°F. Lightly grease a 9-inch springform pan with cooking spray. Stir together the wafer crumbs, melted butter, and 3 tablespoons of sugar in a medium bowl. Press the mixture on the bottom and 1 inch up the sides of prepared pan. Bake at 350°F for 10 minutes. Let stand at room temperature until ready to use.

2. Make the filling: Reduce oven temperature to 325°F. Microwave the chocolate morsels and cream in a small microwave-safe bowl at MEDIUM (50% power) 1 to 1½ minutes or until melted and smooth, stirring at 30-second intervals. Cool 10 minutes.

3. Beat the cream cheese and 1 cup sugar at medium-low speed with a heavy-duty electric stand mixer just until smooth. Add the chocolate mixture and extracts, and beat at low speed just until blended. Add the eggs, 1 at a time, beating at low speed just until yellow disappears after each addition; pour into prepared crust.

4. Bake at 325°F for 50 minutes to 1 hour or until the center of cheesecake jiggles and is almost set. Remove the cheesecake from the oven, and gently run a knife around the outer edge of cheesecake to loosen from the sides of the pan. (Do not remove sides.) Cool the cheesecake completely on a wire rack (about 2 hours). Cover and chill 8 hours to 2 days.

5. Make the peppermint cream: Beat the cream and peppermint extract at medium-high speed until foamy; gradually add powdered sugar, beating until soft peaks form. Remove the sides of the pan, and spread the whipped cream over the top of the cheesecake.

TRIPLE CHOCOLATE BROWNIE-MOUSSE STACKS

Allow plenty of time to make fillings, and immediately assemble stacks.
You can chill the assembled stacks up to 24 hours ahead of time.

SERVES 8 · **HANDS-ON:** 45 minutes · **TOTAL:** 4 hours, 30 minutes

BROWNIES:
Vegetable cooking spray
6   ounces (¾ cup) butter
1   (4-ounce) bittersweet
      dark chocolate baking bar,
      chopped
1½ cups sugar
1   teaspoon vanilla extract
4   large eggs

1   cup (4.5 ounces)
      all-purpose flour
¼   teaspoon baking powder
¼   teaspoon table salt

MILK CHOCOLATE MOUSSE:
1   cup milk chocolate morsels
¼   cup creamy peanut butter
1   cup heavy cream

WHITE CHOCOLATE MOUSSE:
1   cup white chocolate morsels
1¼ cups heavy cream

MOLDS:
8   large paper clips
Heavy-duty aluminum foil
Garnish: shaved chocolate

1. Make the brownies: Preheat the oven to 350°F. Line bottom and sides of a 13- x 9-inch pan with aluminum foil, allowing 2 to 3 inches to extend over sides; lightly grease foil with cooking spray. Microwave the butter and chopped bittersweet chocolate in a large microwave-safe bowl at HIGH 1½ to 2 minutes or just until melted and smooth, stirring at 30-second intervals. Whisk in the sugar and vanilla. Add the eggs, 1 at a time, whisking just until blended after each addition. Stir together the flour, baking powder, and salt in a small bowl. Whisk the flour mixture into the chocolate mixture until blended. Pour into the prepared pan.

2. Bake at 350°F for 18 to 20 minutes or until a wooden pick inserted in center comes out with a few moist crumbs. Cool completely on a wire rack (about 1 hour). Lift brownies from pan, using foil sides as handles. Cut 8 circles, using a 3-inch round cutter. Reserve scraps for another use.

3. Make the milk chocolate mousse: Microwave the milk chocolate morsels and peanut butter in a small microwave-safe glass bowl at MEDIUM (50% power) 1½ to 2 minutes or until melted and smooth, stirring at 30-second intervals. Cool 5 minutes.

4. Beat 1 cup of the heavy cream at medium speed with an electric mixer until soft peaks form; fold cream into milk chocolate mixture. Chill while making the white chocolate mousse.

5. Make the white chocolate mousse: Microwave the white chocolate morsels and ¼ cup of the cream in a small microwave-safe glass bowl at MEDIUM (50% power) 1½ to 2 minutes or until melted and smooth, stirring at 30-second intervals. Cool 5 minutes.

6. Beat remaining 1 cup cream at medium speed with an electric mixer until soft peaks form; fold into white chocolate mixture. Chill while preparing foil molds.

7. Assemble the molds: Wash and dry paper clips. Cut heavy-duty aluminum foil into 8 (10- x 6-inch) pieces. Fold each piece in half to form a 10-inch x 3-inch strip. Wrap each strip around a 3-inch-diameter can. (This helps create a smooth curve.) Wrap 1 curved foil strip around each brownie round; secure foil with a large paper clip. Immediately spoon milk chocolate mousse into a zip-top plastic freezer bag. (Do not seal.) Snip 1 corner of bag to make a small hole (about ½ inch). Pipe mousse onto brownies, dividing mixture evenly. Use a small spoon to level gently. Repeat procedure with white chocolate mousse. Chill 2 hours; remove foil to serve.

SWEET POTATO TARTLETS WITH CRÈME FRAÎCHE TOPPING

*We prefer to bake fresh sweet potatoes to use in these individual tarts,
instead of using canned, because it brings out their natural sweetness. Pureeing them in
a food processor instead of mashing them creates a silkier texture in the filling.*

SERVES 6 · **HANDS-ON:** 25 minutes · **TOTAL:** 3 hours, 48 minutes

1¼ pounds sweet potatoes
(2 medium)

Vegetable cooking spray

1 (7.25-ounce) package
shortbread cookies

⅓ cup toasted sliced almonds

1 tablespoon granulated sugar

2 ounces (¼ cup) butter, melted

1½ cups heavy cream

⅓ cup granulated sugar

⅓ cup firmly packed
dark brown sugar

1 teaspoon vanilla extract

¾ teaspoon ground cinnamon

½ teaspoon table salt

½ teaspoon ground ginger

¼ teaspoon freshly
grated nutmeg

2 large eggs

⅓ cup crème fraîche

2 teaspoons dark brown sugar

Garnishes: toasted pecan halves,
freshly grated nutmeg

1. Preheat the oven to 450°F. Line a small shallow baking pan with aluminum foil. Scrub the sweet potatoes; rinse and pat dry with paper towels. Coat the potatoes with cooking spray, and place in prepared pan. Bake at 450°F for 1 hour or until very tender. Remove from oven; reduce the oven temperature to 350°F. Cool the potatoes on a wire rack (about 30 minutes); peel.

2. Meanwhile, lightly grease 6 (4½- x ¾-inch) round tartlet pans with cooking spray. Process the cookies and next 2 ingredients in a food processor until finely ground. Drizzle the butter over cookie mixture; pulse 5 times or until blended. Press about ⅓ cup of the cookie mixture in the bottom and up the sides of each prepared tartlet pan; place on a baking sheet.

3. Bake at 350°F for 14 minutes or until golden brown. Remove from baking sheet to a wire rack, and cool completely (about 30 minutes).

4. Meanwhile, wipe processor bowl clean with a paper towel. Process the sweet potatoes in food processor 20 to 30 seconds or until smooth and silky, stopping to scrape down sides as needed. Add ¾ cup of the cream and next 8 ingredients; process 15 to 30 seconds or just until blended and smooth, stopping to scrape down sides as needed. Pour mixture evenly into cooled tartlet shells.

5. Bake at 350°F for 23 minutes or just until filling is set. Cool completely on a wire rack (about 1 hour).

6. Beat the crème fraîche, 2 teaspoons dark brown sugar, and remaining ¾ cup heavy cream at high speed with an electric mixer until stiff peaks form. Dollop the topping over the tartlets.

NOTE: We tested with Pepperidge Farm Chessmen Cookies.

COCONUT-CITRUS PAVLOVA

The billowy meringue with its crisp exterior and luscious citrus cream topping is ethereal.

SERVES 12 · **HANDS-ON:** 35 minutes · **TOTAL:** 6 hours, 35 minutes

CITRUS CURD:
- 5 large egg yolks
- ½ cup sugar
- ⅛ teaspoon table salt
- 1 teaspoon firmly packed lemon zest
- 1 teaspoon firmly packed orange zest
- ¼ cup fresh lemon juice
- ¼ cup fresh orange juice
- 3 ounces (6 tablespoons) butter, cut into 6 pieces

MERINGUE:
- Parchment paper
- 1¼ cups sugar
- 1½ tablespoons cornstarch
- 5 large egg whites
- ¼ teaspoon cream of tartar
- ⅛ teaspoon table salt
- ½ teaspoon vanilla extract

TOPPING:
- ¾ cup heavy cream
- 2 cups assorted citrus sections, such as orange, blood orange, grapefruit, and tangerine
- ½ cup shaved fresh coconut, lightly toasted

1. Make the curd: Whisk together first 5 ingredients in a 2-quart saucepan. Whisk in the citrus juices. Cook, whisking, over medium 5 minutes (do not boil). Remove from heat; add butter, 1 tablespoon at a time, until melted and smooth. Pour curd through a wire-mesh strainer into a bowl. Place plastic wrap directly onto surface to prevent a film from forming. Chill 2 to 24 hours.

2. Make the meringue: Preheat the oven to 225°F. Line a baking sheet with parchment paper and draw a 9-inch circle on paper. Whisk together the sugar and cornstarch in a bowl. Beat the egg whites at medium-high speed with a heavy-duty electric stand mixer 1 minute; add the cream of tartar and salt, beating until blended. Gradually add the sugar mixture, 1 tablespoon at a time, beating at medium-high speed until mixture is glossy, stiff peaks form, and sugar dissolves (2 to 4 minutes). (Do not overbeat.) Beat in the vanilla. Gently spread the mixture into the circle on prepared baking sheet, making a large indentation in center of meringue to hold filling.

3. Bake at 225°F for 2 hours or until outside has formed a crust. Turn oven off; let the meringue stand in oven, with door closed, 2 hours or until completely cool and dry.

4. Make the pavlova: Carefully remove the meringue from parchment paper, and place on a serving platter. Beat the heavy cream at high speed with an electric mixer until stiff peaks form; gently fold the whipped cream into curd. Spoon the curd mixture onto center of meringue; top with citrus sections and toasted coconut. Serve immediately.

Milk Punch Tres Leches Cake

MILK PUNCH TRES LECHES CAKE

Bake this a day before serving so it soaks up the creamy syrup. Make mini cakes with a round cutter. Top with whipped cream and a grating of nutmeg.

SERVES 16 · **HANDS-ON:** 45 minutes · **TOTAL:** 13 hours, 20 minutes

Vegetable cooking spray
4 ounces (½ cup) butter, softened
1 cup granulated sugar
7 large eggs, separated
2½ cups (11.25 ounces) all-purpose flour
1½ teaspoons baking powder

½ teaspoon table salt
1 cup milk
1 teaspoon vanilla extract
1 (14-ounce) can sweetened condensed milk
1 (12-ounce) can evaporated milk

½ cup coffee liqueur
1½ cups heavy cream
¾ cup powdered sugar
Garnish: freshly grated nutmeg

1. Preheat the oven to 350°F. Lightly grease a a 13- x 9-inch pan with cooking spray. Beat the butter at medium speed with an electric mixer until creamy; add granulated sugar, beating until light and fluffy. Add the egg yolks, 1 at a time, beating until blended after each addition. Stir together the flour, baking powder, and salt. Add flour mixture to butter mixture alternately with milk, beginning and ending with flour mixture. Beat at low speed until blended after each addition. Stir in vanilla. Wash and dry beaters.

2. Beat the egg whites at high speed until stiff peaks form. Stir about one-third of egg whites into batter; fold in remaining egg whites in 2 batches. Spoon batter into prepared pan.

3. Bake at 350°F for 23 minutes or until a wooden pick inserted in the center comes out clean. Cool in pan on a wire rack 10 minutes.

4. Pierce the top of cake several times with a long wooden pick. Whisk together condensed milk, evaporated milk, and liqueur. Gradually pour mixture over warm cake, about ½ cup at a time. Allow mixture to soak into cake before adding more. Let the cake stand at room temperature for 3 hours. Cover and chill 8 to 12 hours.

5. Beat heavy cream and powdered sugar at medium-high speed with an electric mixer until stiff peaks form; spread on cake.

CHOCOLATE-BANANA BREAD PUDDING

Be sure to use soft ladyfingers found in the bakery department of your grocery store.

SERVES 8 to 10 · **HANDS-ON:** 30 minutes · **TOTAL:** 4 hours, 30 minutes

1 envelope unflavored gelatin
¼ cup cold water
¾ cup granulated sugar
⅓ cup unsweetened cocoa
5 large egg yolks
3½ cups heavy cream

1 teaspoon vanilla extract
1 cup semisweet chocolate mini-morsels
1½ (3-ounce) packages ladyfingers
¼ cup coffee liqueur

¼ cup brewed coffee
4 medium bananas, sliced
Garnish: chocolate curls

1. Sprinkle the gelatin over ¼ cup cold water in a small bowl.

2. Whisk together the sugar and cocoa in a large saucepan until blended. Whisk in the egg yolks and 2 cups of the cream. Cook, whisking constantly, over medium 5 to 6 minutes or until thickened. Remove from heat; stir in gelatin mixture and vanilla, whisking until gelatin dissolves.

3. Fill a large bowl with ice. Place pan containing the custard in ice, and let stand 10 minutes or until custard cools to room temperature, stirring occasionally.

4. Meanwhile, place ½ cup of the mini-morsels in a small microwave-safe bowl; microwave at HIGH 30 to 60 seconds, stirring at 30-second intervals until smooth.

5. Beat remaining 1½ cups heavy cream at high speed with an electric mixer until soft peaks form. Add the melted chocolate and remaining ½ cup mini-morsels to custard, stirring until blended. Gently fold in 2 cups of the whipped cream. Cover and chill remaining whipped cream.

6. Layer half of the ladyfingers in an 8-inch square baking dish. Combine the liqueur and coffee. Brush half of the coffee mixture over ladyfingers in dish. Top with half of the banana slices and half of custard. Repeat procedure with remaining ladyfingers, coffee mixture, banana slices, and custard. Cover and chill 4 hours or until set.

7. Spread remaining 1 cup whipped cream over custard just before serving.

DECADENT CREAM PUFFS WITH PRALINE SAUCE AND TOASTED PECANS

It may be tempting to use a stand mixer for the cream puff batter, but it pays to mix it by hand: You need to see when the mixture is smooth and shiny, which will prevent overmixing.

SERVES 8 · **HANDS-ON:** 30 minutes · **TOTAL:** 1 hour, 25 minutes, including sauce

CREAM PUFFS:
Parchment paper
Vegetable cooking spray
1 cup water
4 ounces (½ cup) butter
1 cup (4.5 ounces) all-purpose flour
⅛ teaspoon table salt
4 large eggs

PRALINE SAUCE:
1 cup firmly packed light brown sugar
½ cup half-and-half
4 ounces (½ cup) butter
Pinch of table salt
1 teaspoon vanilla extract

FILLING AND GARNISH:
4 cups butter-pecan ice cream
1 cup coarsely chopped toasted pecans

1. Make the cream puffs: Preheat the oven to 400°F. Line a baking sheet with parchment paper and lightly grease with cooking spray. Bring 1 cup water to a boil in a large saucepan over medium-high. Reduce heat to low, and add the butter, stirring until melted.

2. Stir in the flour and salt, beating vigorously with a wooden spoon 1 minute or until mixture leaves sides of saucepan. Remove from heat, and cool 5 minutes. Add the eggs, 1 at a time, beating with wooden spoon until smooth. Drop by rounded ¼ cupfuls, 2 inches apart, onto prepared baking sheet.

3. Bake at 400°F for 30 to 35 minutes or until puffed and golden brown. Remove from oven, and, using a wooden pick, poke a small hole into side of each cream puff to allow steam to escape. Cool completely on baking sheet on a wire rack (about 30 minutes).

4. Make the praline sauce: Bring the brown sugar and next 3 ingredients to a boil in a small saucepan over medium, stirring constantly. Cook, stirring constantly, 1 minute. Remove from heat, and stir in vanilla. Let stand 10 minutes. Keep warm.

5. Cut each cream puff in half horizontally; remove and discard any soft dough inside. Spoon ½ cup of the ice cream onto each bottom half; top the cream puffs with remaining halves. Spoon 3 tablespoons of the sauce over each puff; sprinkle with toasted pecans. Serve immediately with remaining warm sauce.

CHERRY-SPICE CAKE TRIFLE

Make the layers ahead of time and freeze until the day before assembly.

SERVES 15 to 20 · **HANDS-ON:** 45 minutes · **TOTAL:** 9 hours, 15 minutes

CAKE:
Shortening
8   ounces (1 cup) butter, softened
1   cup granulated sugar
1   cup firmly packed light brown sugar
4   large eggs
1½ cups cooked, mashed sweet potato
2   teaspoons vanilla extract
3   cups (13.5 ounces) all-purpose flour
1   tablespoon baking powder
1   teaspoon ground cinnamon
½   teaspoon baking soda
½   teaspoon table salt
½   teaspoon ground ginger
¼   teaspoon ground nutmeg
1   cup buttermilk

FILLING:
1   (13-ounce) jar cherry preserves
¾   cup granulated sugar
¼   cup fresh orange juice
4   cups fresh or frozen cranberries

CUSTARD:
1   cup firmly packed light brown sugar
5   tablespoons cornstarch
¼   teaspoon table salt
3½ cups milk
1½ cups heavy cream
2   ounces (¼ cup) butter, cut into pieces
1   teaspoon vanilla bean paste
¼   teaspoon ground cinnamon
⅛   teaspoon ground nutmeg

TOPPING:
2   cups heavy cream
1   teaspoon vanilla extract
6   tablespoons powdered sugar
Garnishes: fresh cranberries, rosemary sprigs

1. Make the cake: Preheat the oven to 350°F. Grease (with shortening) and flour 2 (9-inch) round 2-inch-deep cake pans. Beat the butter at medium speed with a heavy-duty electric stand mixer until creamy. Gradually add the sugars, and beat until light and fluffy. Add the eggs, 1 at a time, beating just until blended after each addition. Add the sweet potato and vanilla, beating just until blended.

2. Stir together the flour and next 6 ingredients. Add to the butter mixture alternately with the buttermilk, beginning and ending with the flour mixture. Beat at low speed just until blended after each addition. Spoon batter into prepared cake pans.

3. Bake at 350°F for 35 to 40 minutes or until a wooden pick inserted in center comes out clean. Cool in pans on a wire rack 10 minutes; remove from pans to wire rack, and cool completely (about 1 hour).

4. Make the filling: Bring the preserves, next 2 ingredients, and 3 cups of the cranberries to a boil in a saucepan over medium-high; reduce heat to low, and boil, stirring often, 5 to 6 minutes or until cranberry skins begin to split. Remove from heat, and stir in remaining 1 cup cranberries. Transfer the mixture to a bowl; cool completely (about 30 minutes). Cover and chill 8 to 24 hours.

5. Meanwhile, make the custard: Whisk together the brown sugar, cornstarch, and salt in a large heavy saucepan; whisk in the milk and 1½ cups cream. Bring the mixture to a boil over medium, whisking constantly. Boil 1 minute, whisking constantly. Remove from heat.

6. Whisk in the butter and next 3 ingredients. Transfer the mixture to a medium bowl, and place plastic wrap directly on mixture (to prevent a film from forming). Cool completely (about 30 minutes). Chill 8 to 24 hours.

7. Make the trifle: Layer about one-third of the cake cubes in a 4-quart bowl. Top with one-third each cranberry filling and custard. Repeat layers twice.

8. Make the topping: Beat 2 cups heavy cream and vanilla at medium-high speed until foamy; gradually add powdered sugar, beating until soft peaks form. Dollop over the trifle. Serve immediately, or chill up to 8 hours.

GINGERBREAD BAKED ALASKA

The bowl from a heavy-duty stand mixer is a perfect mold for assembling this dessert.

SERVES 8 to 10 · **HANDS-ON:** 1 hour · **TOTAL:** 14 hours, 35 minutes

CAKE:
Shortening
2 cups firmly packed
   dark brown sugar
8 ounces (1 cup) butter,
   softened
3 large eggs
1 tablespoon grated
   fresh ginger
1 teaspoon vanilla extract
3 cups (13.5 ounces)
   all-purpose flour
1 teaspoon baking soda
½ teaspoon baking powder

½ teaspoon table salt
¼ teaspoon ground nutmeg
¼ teaspoon ground allspice
1½ cups buttermilk
¼ cup minced
   crystallized ginger
Vegetable cooking spray

ICE CREAM:
½ gallon vanilla ice cream,
   softened
1 tablespoon lemon zest
2 tablespoons fresh
   lemon juice

SWISS MERINGUE:
5 large egg whites
1¼ cups (8.75 ounces)
   granulated sugar
1 teaspoon vanilla extract

1. Make the cake: Preheat the oven to 350°F. Grease (with shortening) and flour 3 (8-inch) round cake pans. Beat brown sugar and butter at medium speed with an electric stand mixer until light and fluffy. Add eggs, 1 at a time, beating just until blended after each addition. Stir in the ginger and vanilla.

2. Whisk together the flour and next 5 ingredients in a small bowl. Add the flour mixture to brown sugar mixture alternately with buttermilk, beginning and ending with flour mixture. Beat at low speed just until blended after each addition. Stir in the crystallized ginger. Spoon batter into prepared cake pans. Bake at 350°F for 23 to 28 minutes or until a wooden pick inserted in center comes out clean. Cool in pans on wire racks 10 minutes. Remove from pans to wire racks, and cool completely (about 1 hour).

3. Cut a 6-inch circle from 1 of the cake layers. (We used a 6-inch round cake pan as a guide.) Reserve scraps for another use. Lightly grease a 5-quart metal bowl with cooking spray. Line bowl with plastic wrap, allowing 4 to 5 inches to extend over sides.

4. Make the ice cream: Stir together the softened ice cream, zest, and lemon juice.

5. Assemble: Spoon 1½ cups of the ice-cream mixture into prepared bowl. Place the 6-inch cake layer on ice-cream mixture, and press gently. Top with half of remaining ice-cream mixture. Place 1 (8-inch) cake layer on ice-cream mixture; press gently. Top with remaining ice-cream mixture and remaining 8-inch cake layer; press gently. Fold extended plastic wrap over cake layer to cover completely. Freeze 12 to 24 hours.

6. Uncover the cake and ice cream, and invert bowl onto a serving platter, keeping plastic wrap around sides and top of cake and ice cream. Return to freezer.

7. Make the meringue: Pour water to a depth of 1½ inches into a small saucepan; bring to a boil over medium-high. Reduce heat to medium-low, and maintain at a simmer. Whisk together the egg whites and 1¼ cups granulated sugar in bowl of a heavy-duty electric stand mixer. Place bowl over simmering water, and cook, whisking constantly, 3 minutes or until sugar dissolves and a candy thermometer registers 140°F. Whisk in 1 teaspoon vanilla.

8. Beat mixture at medium-high speed with an electric stand mixer, using whisk attachment, 8 to 10 minutes or until stiff peaks form and meringue has cooled completely. Remove the cake and ice cream from freezer; remove and discard plastic wrap. Spread the meringue over top and sides, completely covering cake and ice cream. Brown the meringue using a kitchen torch, holding torch 2 inches from meringue and moving torch back and forth. Serve immediately.

GINGERBREAD ROULADE

This cake roll is easier to slice when chilled, but it tastes best when eaten at room temperature.

SERVES 8 to 10 • **HANDS-ON:** 35 minutes • **TOTAL:** 3 hours, 47 minutes

CAKE:
Vegetable cooking spray
Parchment paper
Shortening
⅔ cup cake flour
1½ teaspoons ground cinnamon
1½ teaspoons ground ginger
½ teaspoon baking powder
¼ teaspoon table salt
¼ teaspoon ground cloves
¼ teaspoon ground allspice
4 large eggs, separated

½ cup granulated sugar
3 tablespoons molasses
3 tablespoons butter, melted
1 teaspoon vanilla extract
⅓ cup powdered sugar

SYRUP:
¼ cup granulated sugar
¼ cup water
2 tablespoons ginger liqueur or brandy

FROSTING:
1 cup heavy cream
2 tablespoons brandy
1 (8-ounce) container mascarpone cheese, softened
¼ cup powdered sugar
⅛ teaspoon table salt
Chopped crystallized ginger
Garnish: White Chocolate Snowflakes

1. Make the cake: Preheat the oven to 400°F. Grease a 15- x 10-inch jelly-roll pan with cooking spray, and line with parchment paper. Grease parchment paper with shortening, and dust with flour.

2. Whisk together the cake flour and next 6 ingredients in a medium bowl. Beat the egg yolks and ¼ cup of the granulated sugar at high speed with an electric mixer until thick and pale. Reduce speed to low. Beat in the molasses, butter, and vanilla. Sift the flour mixture over egg yolk mixture, in 3 additions, gently folding in flour mixture after each addition.

3. Thoroughly clean beaters. Beat the egg whites at medium speed with an electric mixer until foamy; add remaining ¼ cup granulated sugar, beating until stiff peaks form and sugar dissolves (3 minutes). Gently fold the egg white mixture into batter. Gently spread the batter in prepared pan.

4. Bake at 400°F for 10 minutes until browned and a pick inserted in center comes out clean.

5. Sprinkle ⅓ cup powdered sugar over top of cake. Invert the cake onto a parchment paper-lined surface. Peel top layer of parchment from cake. Starting at 1 short side, immediately roll the cake and bottom parchment paper together. Cool completely (about 1 hour).

6. Make the syrup: Combine the sugar and ¼ cup water in a saucepan over medium-high. Bring to a simmer, stirring until sugar dissolves. Remove from heat; cool 5 minutes. Stir in liqueur.

7. Make the frosting: Beat the cream and brandy at high speed with an electric mixer until stiff peaks form. Stir together the mascarpone, powdered sugar, and salt in a separate bowl until blended. Gently fold the whipped cream mixture into mascarpone mixture until blended. Reserve 1½ cups of the frosting; cover and chill for later use.

8. Unroll the cake onto a flat surface. Poke holes all over the cake with a wooden pick. Brush the syrup onto cake in several additions, letting syrup soak into cake after each addition. Spread remaining 1½ cups frosting over cake, leaving a 1-inch border on all sides. Lift and tilt parchment paper, and roll up the cake in jelly-roll fashion, starting at 1 short side and using parchment paper as a guide. Place the cake, wrapped in parchment paper, on a baking sheet. Chill 2 to 24 hours.

9. Transfer the cake to a serving platter; remove and discard parchment paper. Top with the reserved chilled frosting; sprinkle with crystallized ginger.

FOR WHITE CHOCOLATE SNOWFLAKES: Line a baking sheet with parchment paper. Melt 4 ounces chopped white chocolate in a small microwave-safe bowl on HIGH 1 to 1½ minutes, stirring at 30-second intervals. Spoon into a piping bag fitted with a #3 plain tip. Pipe the snowflake patterns onto a parchment paper-lined baking sheet. Refrigerate 30 minutes or until set. Carefully remove from parchment, and place on the cake. Snowflake stencils can also be printed from the Internet.

CHOCOLATE-PEPPERMINT LAYER CAKE

This decadent dessert combines the rich flavor of chocolate with a holiday staple: peppermint. It's the perfect ending to your holiday meal. Garnish the cake with cake decorations from the pastry supply store.

SERVES 12 to 16 · **HANDS-ON:** 30 minutes · **TOTAL:** 2 hours, 15 minutes

CAKE:
Shortening
Parchment paper
2 cups granulated sugar
2 cups (9 ounces) all-purpose flour
1 teaspoon baking soda
½ teaspoon table salt
8 ounces (1 cup) unsalted butter
¼ cup unsweetened dark cocoa
1 cup water

3 ounces bittersweet chocolate, chopped
½ cup buttermilk
2 large eggs, lightly beaten
1 teaspoon vanilla extract

PEPPERMINT BUTTERCREAM FROSTING:
12 ounces (1½ cups) unsalted butter, softened
8 cups powdered sugar, sifted
1 teaspoon vanilla extract

½ teaspoon peppermint extract
⅛ teaspoon table salt
¼ cup heavy cream
½ cup crushed peppermint stick candies
2 drops of red liquid food coloring
Garnishes: red and white candies, red and white chocolate curls, red and white snowflakes

1. Make the cake: Preheat the oven to 350°F. Grease 2 (8-inch) round cake pans with shortening. Line the pans with parchment paper; grease the parchment paper, and dust with flour.

2. Combine the granulated sugar, flour, baking soda, and salt in a large bowl. Bring the butter, cocoa, and 1 cup water to a boil in a small saucepan over medium-high, whisking often until butter melts. Add the chocolate, whisking until melted. Whisk the butter mixture into flour mixture until blended. Add the buttermilk, eggs, and vanilla; whisk until blended. Pour the batter into prepared pans.

3. Bake at 350°F for 30 to 35 minutes or until a wooden pick inserted in center comes out clean. Cool in pans on wire racks 10 minutes. Remove from pans. Cool completely on wire racks (about 1 hour). Cut the layers in half horizontally.

4. Make the frosting: Beat the butter at medium speed with an electric mixer until creamy. Gradually add the powdered sugar, beating at low speed until blended. Beat in the vanilla, peppermint extract, and salt. Add the cream; beat at medium speed 1 minute or until smooth. Transfer 2¼ cups of the frosting to a bowl. Stir in the crushed peppermint candies and red food coloring; spread ¾ cup tinted frosting between layers. Spread remaining 3¼ cups white frosting on top and sides of cake.

NOTE: We tested with Hershey's Special Dark Cocoa.

Hazelnut Brittle and Butterscotch-Pecan Pretzel Brittle, page 183

Red Velvet Moon Pies and Tropical White Chocolate Fudge, page 184

Raspberry Marshmallows, page 178

Mississippi Medallions, page 175

GIFTS
FROM THE
KITCHEN

*Give a gift from the heart with these scratch-made treats
sure to be savored by friends and family alike.*

COCONUT SNOWBALLS

If the melted white chocolate is too firm after it's heated, stir in about ¼ teaspoon of coconut oil.

MAKES about 2 dozen · **HANDS-ON:** 10 minutes · **TOTAL:** 1 hour, 5 minutes

Parchment paper
4 ounces (½ cup) unsalted butter, softened
½ cup powdered sugar
1 teaspoon pure coconut extract or vanilla extract

1 cup (4.5 ounces) all-purpose flour
½ cup unsweetened shredded coconut

4 ounces white chocolate, chopped and melted according to package directions
Garnish: shaved coconut

1. Preheat the oven to 400°F. Line 2 baking sheets with parchment paper. Beat the butter and sugar at medium speed with an electric mixer until creamy. Add the extract; beat 30 seconds. Gradually add the flour, beating at low speed until combined after each addition. Stir in the shredded coconut. (If dough is soft, divide in half, and chill 30 minutes to 5 days.)

2. Drop the dough by level spoonfuls about 2 inches apart onto prepared baking sheets, using a 1-inch cookie scoop.

3. Bake, in batches, at 400°F for 7 to 9 minutes or until golden brown on bottom. Cool completely on a wire rack (about 30 minutes). Spread each cooled cookie with ½ teaspoon of the melted chocolate.

HIDDEN KISS COOKIES

We love making these cookies with mint kisses and candy cane kisses during the holidays.

MAKES 3½ dozen · **HANDS-ON:** 1 hour · **TOTAL:** 1 hour, 30 minutes

Parchment paper
2¼ cups (10.1 ounces) all-purpose flour
1 cup sliced almonds

⅔ cup powdered sugar
½ teaspoon table salt
10 ounces (1¼ cups) butter, softened

1 teaspoon vanilla extract
¼ teaspoon almond extract
42 chocolate kisses

1. Preheat the oven to 350°F. Line 2 baking sheets with parchment paper. Pulse first 4 ingredients in a food processor until almonds are finely ground.

2. Beat butter together with vanilla extract and almond extract at medium-high speed with an electric mixer about 30 seconds or until creamy. Add flour mixture in 2 batches, beating until blended after each addition. Turn dough out onto a lightly floured surface, and knead 4 to 5 times. Divide dough in half.

3. Working with 1 dough portion, drop by heaping teaspoonfuls 1 inch apart on prepared pans. Press 1 chocolate kiss into center of each cookie. Working with remaining dough portion, cover each chocolate kiss with another heaping teaspoonful of dough. Pinch top and bottom edges of dough together to seal.

4. Bake at 350°F for 15 minutes, placing 1 baking sheet on middle oven rack and 1 sheet on lower oven rack. Rotate pans front to back and top rack to bottom rack. Bake 3 to 5 more minutes or until edges of cookies just begin to brown. Cool cookies on parchment paper on wire racks 10 minutes. Sprinkle with additional powdered sugar.

GERMAN CHOCOLATE CAKE TRUFFLES

Make and cool the German chocolate cake the night before for faster day-of assembly.

MAKES 8½ dozen • **HANDS-ON:** 30 minutes • **TOTAL:** 2 hours

Vegetable cooking spray
1 (18.25-ounce) package
   German chocolate cake mix
Wax paper
1 (16-ounce) container milk
   chocolate ready-to-spread
   frosting

2 cups toasted coconut
1¾ cups toasted finely
   chopped pecans
4 (7-ounce) containers milk
   chocolate dipping chocolate

Candy dipping fork
Paper or aluminum foil
   baking cups

1. Lightly grease a 13- x 9-inch pan with cooking spray. Prepare the cake mix according to package directions and bake in the prepared pan. Cool completely in pan (about 30 minutes).

2. Line baking sheets with wax paper. Crumble cake into a large bowl. Scoop frosting by spoonfuls over cake crumbs. Sprinkle with 1 cup each of the coconut and pecans; stir gently just until thoroughly blended. Using a cookie scoop, scoop cake mixture into 1¼-inch balls; roll in hands, and place balls (spaced evenly apart) on prepared baking sheets. Cover and chill 1 hour.

3. While the cake balls chill, combine remaining 1 cup coconut and ¾ cup pecans; stir well. Melt the dipping chocolate, 1 container at a time, according to package directions; dip the chilled balls into melted chocolate, using candy dipping fork and allowing excess chocolate to drip off. Place the coated truffles on wax paper-lined baking sheets. Sprinkle the tops with coconut-pecan mixture; chill 30 minutes or until set. Place the truffles in baking cups.

Red Velvet
Thumbprints

Pecan-Cranberry
Shortbread

RED VELVET THUMBPRINTS

Transfer the frosting to a zip-top plastic freezer bag, snip a corner, and pipe. No pastry bag required.

MAKES about 2 dozen • **HANDS-ON:** 12 minutes • **TOTAL:** 1 hour, 20 minutes

Parchment paper
4 ounces (½ cup) unsalted butter, softened
¾ cup granulated sugar
1 large egg
1½ teaspoons red liquid food coloring

1¼ cups (5⅜ ounces) all-purpose flour
1 tablespoon unsweetened cocoa
½ teaspoon table salt
1 teaspoon vanilla extract

2 ounces cream cheese, softened
¼ cup white chocolate morsels, melted according to package directions and cooled
Garnish: white chocolate morsels

1. Preheat the oven to 325°F. Line baking sheets with parchment paper. Beat the butter and sugar at medium speed with an electric mixer until creamy. Add the egg and food coloring; beat 30 seconds.

2. Sift the flour with next 2 ingredients in a small bowl. Add the flour mixture to butter mixture, beating at low speed until combined. Stir in the vanilla.

3. Shape dough into 1-inch balls, and place ½ inch apart on prepared baking sheets. Press thumb or end of a wooden spoon into each ball, forming an indentation.

4. Bake at 325°F for 10 to 15 minutes or until cookies are fragrant and dry. While cookies are still warm, press indentations again. Cool cookies completely on a wire rack (about 30 minutes).

5. Stir together cream cheese and melted white chocolate in a small bowl. Fill centers of cookies with cream cheese mixture.

PECAN-CRANBERRY SHORTBREAD

Making shortbread with melted butter skips the wait for it to soften.

MAKES 8 to 10 cookies • **HANDS-ON:** 10 minutes • **TOTAL:** 1 hour, 40 minutes

Vegetable cooking spray
Parchment paper
¾ cup toasted pecan halves
1 cup powdered sugar
5 ounces (10 tablespoons) unsalted butter, melted

½ cup dried sweetened cranberries
½ teaspoon orange zest
¼ teaspoon table salt
1 cup (4.5 ounces) all-purpose flour

¼ cup semisweet chocolate morsels
½ teaspoon shortening

1. Preheat the oven to 325°F. Lightly grease a 9-inch tart pan with removable bottom with cooking spray. Line a baking sheet with parchment paper. Process ½ cup of the pecans in a food processor until finely ground. Add the powdered sugar and next 4 ingredients; pulse until cranberries are coarsely chopped. Add the flour, and pulse just until combined.

2. Spread the dough in prepared tart pan; press remaining ¼ cup pecans into dough.

3. Bake at 325°F for 30 to 35 minutes or until edges are golden. Remove sides of pan, and cut the shortbread into 8 or 10 wedges. Transfer the wedges to prepared baking sheet. Bake at 325°F for 10 minutes or until firm. Transfer the wedges to a wire rack, and cool completely (about 30 minutes).

4. Microwave the chocolate morsels and shortening in a microwave-safe bowl at HIGH 1 minute or until melted and smooth, stirring halfway through. Drizzle the melted chocolate over cookies; let cookies stand 10 minutes or until chocolate is set.

ALMOND-COCONUT SWIRL CHOCOLATE BARK

Have fun experimenting with cool patterns when creating the chocolate swirl.

MAKES 1¾ pounds · **HANDS-ON:** 9 minutes · **TOTAL:** 39 minutes

Parchment paper
3 cups bittersweet chocolate morsels
8 ounces white chocolate, chopped

⅓ cup sweetened flaked coconut, toasted
⅓ cup chopped natural almonds, toasted

⅓ cup chopped dried cherries

1. Line a baking sheet with parchment paper. Place the bittersweet chocolate morsels in a microwave-safe bowl. Microwave at HIGH 1½ minutes or until melted and smooth, stirring at 30-second intervals. Using an offset spatula, spread the melted chocolate into a 12- x 11-inch rectangle, about ¼ inch thick, on prepared pan.

2. Place the white chocolate in a microwave-safe bowl. Microwave at HIGH 1 minute or until melted, stirring at 15-second intervals until smooth. Spread the white chocolate over bittersweet chocolate. Gently swirl the chocolates using a skewer or the tip of a sharp knife.

3. Sprinkle the coconut, almonds, and dried cherries over chocolate. Chill 30 minutes or until firm. Break into large chunks. Store in an airtight container.

CANDY CANE LANE SNACK MIX

Package in red-and-white striped containers lined with clear cellophane for a fun presentation.

MAKES 3 pounds · **HANDS-ON:** 15 minutes · **TOTAL:** 35 minutes

Vegetable cooking spray
Parchment paper
7 cups unsalted popped popcorn
3 cups mini-pretzel twists
2 cups shelled salted pistachios

1¼ pounds vanilla candy coating, coarsely chopped
½ cup finely crushed red peppermint candy canes

1 cup white chocolate-peppermint baking chips
1 (5.8-ounce) container candy cane sprinkles

1. Grease a large bowl with cooking spray. Line 2 jelly-roll pans with parchment paper. Remove the unpopped kernels from popcorn. Combine the popcorn, pretzel twists, and pistachios in the prepared bowl.

2. Place the candy coating in a medium saucepan. Cook over low 3 to 5 minutes or until the coating melts, stirring occasionally. Stir in the crushed peppermint candy. Pour the melted candy mixture over popcorn mixture; toss to coat using 2 spatulas coated with cooking spray. Divide the mixture between prepared jelly-roll pans. Sprinkle with the white chocolate-peppermint baking chips, pressing gently to adhere. Top with the candy cane sprinkles. Let stand 20 minutes or until firm. Break into pieces. Store in an airtight container in a cool place.

NOTE: We used Andes Peppermint Crunch Baking Chips.

**Candy Cane Lane
Snack Mix**

**Almond-Coconut Swirl
Chocolate Bark**

MISSISSIPPI MEDALLIONS

Feel free to substitute mini marshmallows for the espresso beans for a slightly tamer treat.

MAKES 3 dozen · **HANDS-ON:** 25 minutes · **TOTAL:** 40 minutes

Parchment paper
6 whole graham crackers

2 cups semisweet chocolate morsels
⅔ cup pecan halves, toasted

¼ cup chocolate-covered espresso beans

1. Line a baking sheet with parchment paper. Place 3 whole graham crackers in a zip-top plastic freezer bag, and roll with a rolling pin until finely crushed. Spoon crushed graham crackers by level ½ teaspoonfuls 1 inch apart onto the prepared pan; flatten into 1-inch rounds. Break remaining crackers into ½-inch pieces.

2. Microwave chocolate morsels in a microwave-safe bowl at HIGH 30 seconds; stir. Microwave 10 to 20 more seconds or until melted and smooth, stirring at 10-second intervals.

3. Spoon melted chocolate into a large zip-top plastic freezer bag. Snip 1 corner of bag to make a small hole. Pipe chocolate over each graham cracker round.

4. Working quickly, press 1 (½-inch) graham cracker piece, 1 toasted pecan, and 1 espresso bean onto each chocolate round. Chill 15 minutes. Store in an airtight container at room temperature up to 1 week.

COOKIE PRESS SANDWICHES

Pick your favorite filling for this classic sandwich cookie: We tested with peppermint, orange, and lemon extracts and used food coloring to match each flavor.

MAKES 3 dozen • **HANDS-ON:** 2 hours • **TOTAL:** 2 hours, 45 minutes

- 8 ounces (1 cup) butter, softened
- ½ cup granulated sugar
- ½ teaspoon almond extract
- ½ teaspoon vanilla extract
- 1 large egg
- 2¼ cups (10.1 ounces) all-purpose flour

- ½ teaspoon table salt
- 4 ounces (½ cup) butter, softened
- 1 (16-ounce) package powdered sugar
- 3 to 4 tablespoons milk

- ¾ teaspoon flavored extract (such as peppermint, lemon, or orange)
- Food coloring
- ½ cup powdered sugar

1. Preheat the oven to 400°F. Beat first 4 ingredients at medium speed with an electric mixer 1 minute. Add egg, and beat 30 seconds.

2. Sift together flour and salt. Add flour mixture to butter mixture, and beat at low speed 30 seconds. Scrape sides of bowl, and beat 15 more seconds. Divide dough into 3 equal portions.

3. Following manufacturer's instructions, use a cookie press fitted with desired disk to shape dough into cookies, spacing cookies 1½ inches apart on 2 ungreased baking sheets.

4. Bake at 400°F for 7 minutes, placing 1 baking sheet on middle oven rack and 1 sheet on lower oven rack. Rotate baking sheets front to back and top rack to bottom rack. Bake 1 to 2 more minutes or until golden brown around edges. Transfer cookies to a wire rack, and cool completely (about 10 minutes). Repeat with remaining dough.

5. Beat ½ cup butter and next 2 ingredients at medium speed 2 minutes. Add flavored extract; beat at low speed until blended. Add desired amount of food coloring; beat at low speed until blended.

6. Spoon filling into a zip-top plastic freezer bag. (Do not seal.) Snip 1 corner of bag to make a small hole. Pipe filling onto bottom of 1 cookie. Top with a second cookie, so bottom sides of both cookies touch filling. Repeat with remaining cookies and filling. Sprinkle with powdered sugar. Serve immediately, or let stand 2 hours. Store in an airtight container up to 2 weeks.

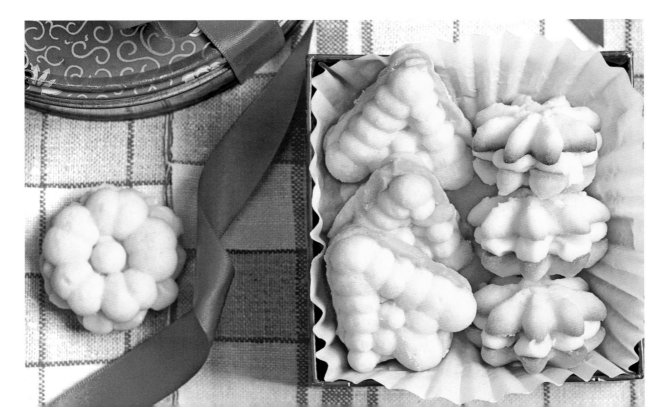

CHEWY DARK CHOCOLATE-WALNUT COOKIES

These cookies will be lovely gifts for the holidays. Be sure to include the recipe because your friends will want to make them too.

MAKES about 8 dozen • **HANDS-ON:** 40 minutes • **TOTAL:** 1 hour, 33 minutes

Parchment paper
2 cups granulated sugar
4 ounces (½ cup) butter, softened
2 ounces (¼ cup) shortening
2 large eggs

2 teaspoons vanilla extract
2 cups (9 ounces) all-purpose flour
¾ cup unsweetened cocoa
1 teaspoon baking soda
½ teaspoon table salt

1 (10-ounce) package dark chocolate morsels
1½ cups chopped walnut pieces
2 cups vanilla candy coating
½ cup sparkling sugar

1. Preheat the oven to 350°F. Line baking sheets with parchment paper. Combine the sugar and next 2 ingredients in a bowl; beat at medium speed with an electric mixer until fluffy. Add the eggs and vanilla, beating until blended.

2. Whisk together the flour and next 3 ingredients. Gradually add the flour mixture to butter mixture, beating at low speed until blended. Stir in the chocolate morsels and walnuts.

3. Drop dough by 1½ teaspoonfuls onto prepared baking sheets. Bake at 350°F for 10 to 12 minutes. Transfer the cookies to wire racks; cool completely (20 minutes).

4. Place the candy coating in a microwave-safe bowl. Microwave at HIGH 1 minute, stirring at 15-second intervals until smooth. Cool the melted candy slightly; spoon candy into a zip-top plastic freezer bag (do not seal). Snip 1 corner of bag to make a small hole. Drizzle the melted candy over cooled cookies, and immediately sprinkle with the sparkling sugar.

RASPBERRY MARSHMALLOWS

*These raspberry-flavored marshmallows are delicious in hot chocolate, or drizzled
with melted bittersweet chocolate before packaging for an even more swoon-worthy sweet. Cut into
shapes using lightly greased cookie cutters and reserve any scraps for your own cup of cocoa.*

MAKES about 4½ dozen • **HANDS-ON:** 31 minutes • **TOTAL:** 12 hours, 36 minutes

Vegetable cooking spray
¾   cup fresh raspberries
½   cup plus 2 tablespoons
     powdered sugar

1   cup cold water
3   envelopes unflavored gelatin
2   cups granulated sugar
⅔   cup light corn syrup

¼   teaspoon table salt
1   teaspoon vanilla extract
½   cup cornstarch

1. Line bottom and sides of a 13- x 9-inch pan with aluminum foil, allowing 2 to 3 inches to extend
over sides; lightly grease with cooking spray.

2. Process the raspberries and 2 tablespoons of the powdered sugar in a blender or food
processor until smooth, stopping to scrape down sides as needed. Pour the raspberry mixture
through a wire-mesh strainer into a bowl using the back of a spoon to squeeze out juice.
Discard pulp and seeds.

3. Place ½ cup of the cold water in bowl of a heavy-duty electric stand mixer fitted with the whisk
attachment. Sprinkle the gelatin over the water; let stand 5 minutes.

4. Combine the granulated sugar, corn syrup, salt, and remaining ½ cup cold water in a medium
saucepan. Bring to a boil over medium, stirring occasionally until sugar dissolves. Cook, without
stirring, until a candy thermometer registers 240°F (soft ball stage), about 6 minutes. Remove
from heat.

5. With mixer on low speed, slowly pour the hot syrup in a thin stream over gelatin mixture.
Increase speed to medium-high, and beat until very thick and stiff, about 8 minutes. Beat in
the raspberry puree and vanilla. Quickly pour the marshmallow mixture into prepared pan,
smoothing top with a lightly greased spatula.

6. Combine remaining ½ cup powdered sugar and cornstarch in a small bowl. Dust top of
the marshmallow mixture in pan with about ⅓ cup of the powdered sugar mixture. Let the
marshmallows stand, uncovered, 12 hours or overnight.

7. Lift the marshmallows from pan using foil sides as handles; flip over onto a cutting board.
Gently remove foil. Dust the marshmallows with ⅓ cup of the powdered sugar mixture.
Cut into 1½-inch squares using a lightly greased knife. Dust cut sides of the marshmallows
with remaining powdered sugar mixture, shaking off excess.

CHOCOLATE-DIPPED GRAHAM CRACKERS

For an extra-special touch to your gift, sprinkle graham crackers with the recipient's favorite chopped nuts or candies immediately after dipping the crackers in chocolate.

MAKES 6 dozen • **HANDS-ON:** 33 minutes • **TOTAL:** 3 hours, 27 minutes

Parchment paper
1½ cups (6.75 ounces) all-purpose flour
1¼ cups whole-wheat flour
⅔ cup firmly packed dark brown sugar

1 teaspoon baking soda
½ teaspoon table salt
6 ounces (¾ cup) cold butter, cut up
3 tablespoons honey
3 tablespoons milk

½ teaspoon vanilla extract
4 (4-ounce) semisweet chocolate baking bars, chopped
Wax paper

1. Line a large baking sheet with parchment paper. Process all-purpose flour and next 4 ingredients in a food processor until blended. Add the butter; pulse 10 times or until mixture resembles coarse meal. Add the honey, milk, and vanilla; process 30 seconds or until dough forms a ball. Divide the dough in half; shape each half into a 4-inch square, and wrap in plastic wrap. Chill 1 hour.

2. Preheat the oven to 350°F. Roll 1 portion of dough into a 12-inch square; cut into 36 (2-inch) squares. Place the squares on prepared pan. Score each square crosswise down center; prick squares several times with a fork.

3. Bake at 350°F for 14 minutes or until bottoms and edges are golden brown and crackers are set. Cool on pan 5 minutes. Transfer the crackers to a wire rack. Cool completely (about 15 minutes). Meanwhile, repeat procedure with remaining portion of dough.

4. Place the chopped chocolate in a microwave-safe bowl. Microwave at HIGH 1 minute or until chocolate melts, stirring every 15 seconds.

5. Dip half of each cracker in the melted chocolate. Place dipped crackers on a work surface lined with wax paper. Let stand 1 hour or until the chocolate is set.

Chocolate-Dipped Graham Crackers and Salted Butterscotch Caramels

SALTED BUTTERSCOTCH CARAMELS

Wrap these decadently sweet bites in wax paper squares to give as gifts.

MAKES 5 dozen • **HANDS-ON:** 34 minutes • **TOTAL:** 2 hours, 34 minutes

Vegetable cooking spray
1 cup heavy cream
1 teaspoon white vinegar
¾ teaspoon fine sea salt, divided

1 tablespoon vanilla extract
6 ounces (¾ cup) butter
1 cup granulated sugar

¾ cup firmly packed brown sugar
Wax paper

1. Line an 8-inch square pan with aluminum foil, allowing 2 to 3 inches to extend over sides. Lightly grease foil with cooking spray.

2. Bring the heavy cream, vinegar, and ½ teaspoon of the salt to a simmer in a medium saucepan over low. Remove from heat, and stir in the vanilla.

3. Combine the butter and next 2 ingredients in a 3-quart heavy saucepan. Cook over medium 10 minutes or until sugar caramelizes and a candy thermometer registers 246°F (firm ball stage), whisking just until sugars dissolve.

4. Remove pan from heat. Whisk in the cream mixture until smooth. Return pan to heat, and cook, without stirring, until thermometer registers 246°F (firm ball stage). Pour the caramel into prepared pan. Sprinkle with remaining ¼ teaspoon salt. Cool completely in pan on a wire rack (about 2 hours).

5. Remove the caramel from pan; discard foil. Cut the caramel into 1-inch squares. Wrap each square in wax paper, and store at room temperature.

PRALINE PECAN GRANOLA WITH APPLES

Granola is easy to prepare and yields a large amount, which makes it perfect for gift giving.

MAKES 6½ cups • **HANDS-ON:** 38 minutes • **TOTAL:** 1 hour, 38 minutes

Vegetable cooking spray
4 ounces (½ cup) butter, melted
⅓ cup honey
3 tablespoons brown sugar

1 teaspoon vanilla extract
½ teaspoon table salt
3 cups uncooked regular oats
2 cups coarsely chopped commercial praline pecans

¼ cup raw wheat germ
¼ cup roasted, salted, and shelled pepitas (pumpkin seeds)
1½ cups chopped dried apples

1. Preheat the oven to 325°F. Lightly grease a 15- x 10-inch jelly-roll pan with cooking spray. Stir together the melted butter and next 4 ingredients in a large bowl. Add the oats and next 3 ingredients, stirring until mixture is coated. Spread the oat mixture on prepared pan.

2. Bake at 325°F for 30 to 35 minutes or until golden brown, stirring every 10 minutes. Stir in the apples. Cool completely in pan on a wire rack (about 30 minutes). Transfer to an airtight container, and store at room temperature.

NOTE: We tested with Hoody's Deep South Praline Pecans.

**Butterscotch-Pecan
Pretzel Brittle**

Hazelnut Brittle

BUTTERSCOTCH-PECAN PRETZEL BRITTLE

This crispy, salty, sweet snack is sure to become a family holiday favorite.

MAKES about 1 pound • **HANDS-ON:** 8 minutes • **TOTAL:** 50 minutes

Parchment paper
5 cups mini-pretzel twists
⅔ cup butterscotch morsels

1 cup chopped pecans
2 ounces (¼ cup) unsalted butter

¼ cup maple syrup
¼ cup sugar

1. Preheat the oven to 350°F. Line an 18- x 13-inch rimmed baking sheet with parchment paper. Place pretzel twists, butterscotch morsels, and ⅔ cup of the pecans in a medium bowl.
2. Combine the butter, syrup, and sugar in a small saucepan. Cook, stirring constantly, over medium 3 to 4 minutes or until butter melts and sugar dissolves. Pour over the pretzel mixture, tossing to coat. Spread the coated pretzel mixture in an even layer on prepared pan (pretzels will overlap). Sprinkle with remaining ⅓ cup pecans.
3. Bake at 350°F for 12 minutes or until lightly browned. Cool completely (about 30 minutes). Break into pieces.

HAZELNUT BRITTLE

Old-fashioned peanut brittle is updated and modernized in this recipe with hazelnuts and sea salt. Drizzle with dark or milk chocolate for an especially rich treat.

MAKES about 1¼ pounds • **HANDS-ON:** 23 minutes • **TOTAL:** 38 minutes

Shortening
1 cup sugar
⅓ cup light corn syrup
¼ cup water

1½ cups roasted skinned hazelnuts, coarsely chopped
2 tablespoons butter
1 teaspoon vanilla extract

½ teaspoon baking soda
½ teaspoon coarse sea salt

1. Grease a 15- x 10-inch jelly-roll pan with shortening. Bring the sugar, corn syrup, and ¼ cup water to a boil over medium in a large heavy saucepan, stirring just until sugar dissolves. Boil, without stirring, 6 minutes or until a candy thermometer registers 270°F (soft crack stage). Stir in the hazelnuts, and cook 3 minutes or until thermometer registers 300°F (hard crack stage). Remove from heat, and stir in the butter, next 2 ingredients, and ¼ teaspoon of the sea salt.
2. Working quickly, spread the mixture in a thin layer in prepared pan. Sprinkle with remaining ¼ teaspoon sea salt. Let stand 15 minutes or until hardened. Break into pieces.

RED VELVET MOON PIES

This handheld version of the classic cake is a treat for children of all ages.

MAKES 18 moon pies · **HANDS-ON:** 30 minutes · **TOTAL:** 1 hour

RED VELVET MOON PIES:
Parchment paper
2¾ cups (12.4 ounces)
    all-purpose flour
⅓ cup unsweetened cocoa
1½ teaspoons baking powder
½ teaspoon baking soda
¼ teaspoon table salt

8 ounces (1 cup) butter,
    softened
1¼ cups granulated sugar
2 large eggs
2 tablespoons red liquid
    food coloring
1 tablespoon vanilla extract
¾ cup buttermilk

MARSHMALLOW FILLING:
4 ounces (½ cup) butter,
    softened
1 cup sifted powdered sugar
1 cup marshmallow crème
½ teaspoon vanilla extract

1. Make the moon pies: Preheat the oven to 350°F. Line baking sheets with parchment paper. Combine flour and next 4 ingredients in a medium bowl.

2. Beat the butter at medium speed with an electric mixer 2 minutes or until creamy. Gradually add the granulated sugar, beating well. Add the eggs, 1 at a time, beating until blended after each addition. Beat in the food coloring and vanilla.

3. Add the flour mixture alternately with buttermilk, beginning and ending with flour mixture. Beat at low speed until blended after each addition, stopping to scrape bowl as needed.

4. Drop the dough by tablespoonfuls onto prepared baking sheets. Spread the dough into 2-inch rounds.

5. Bake at 350°F for 15 minutes or until tops are set. Cool on baking sheets 5 minutes. Remove to wire racks, and cool completely (about 20 minutes).

6. Make the filling: Beat the butter at medium speed with an electric mixer until creamy; gradually add the powdered sugar, beating well. Add the marshmallow crème and vanilla, beating until well blended. Spread the filling onto flat side of each cookie. Join cookies together to make moon pies.

TROPICAL WHITE CHOCOLATE FUDGE

Treat your guests to a taste of the tropics, or give as a gift for fans of fudge with a twist.

MAKES 5 dozen · **HANDS-ON:** 21 minutes · **TOTAL:** 2 hours, 21 minutes

Vegetable cooking spray
4 ounces (½ cup) butter
2 cups sugar
¾ cup sour cream
3 (4-ounce) white chocolate
    baking bars, chopped

1 (7-ounce) jar
    marshmallow crème
½ cup dried apricots, chopped
½ cup dried pineapple,
    chopped

¾ cup chopped
    macadamia nuts
½ cup toasted sweetened
    shredded coconut

1. Line a 9-inch square pan with foil, extending 3 inches over sides; grease with cooking spray.

2. Bring the butter, sugar, and sour cream to a boil in a saucepan over medium. Cook, stirring, 5 minutes or until a thermometer registers 234°F. Remove from heat; stir in chocolate and marshmallow crème until melted. Fold in dried fruit and nuts; pour evenly into the pan. Sprinkle with coconut. Cool in pan (2 hours). Lift fudge by foil edges. Remove foil; cut fudge into 64 squares.

Red Velvet Moon Pies

Tropical White Chocolate Fudge

CRISPY ESPRESSO BROWNIE DELIGHTS

These two-layer brownie treats are chewy and crispy. Be sure to sprinkle the espresso beans quickly over the melted chocolate before it has a chance to harden.

MAKES 30 · **HANDS-ON:** 22 minutes · **TOTAL:** 3 hours, 2 minutes

Vegetable cooking spray

1 (18.75-ounce) package chocolate supreme brownie mix with chocolate syrup

⅓ cup vegetable oil

2 teaspoons instant espresso granules

1 large egg

¼ cup water

3 tablespoons butter

1 (10-ounce) package miniature marshmallows

1 (7-ounce) jar marshmallow crème

6 cups chocolate-flavored crisp rice cereal

3 ounces bittersweet chocolate, chopped

3 ounces white chocolate, chopped

½ cup coarsely crushed chocolate-covered espresso beans

1. Preheat the oven to 325°F. Line 2 (9-inch) square pans with aluminum foil, allowing 2 to 3 inches to extend over sides. Lightly grease foil with cooking spray.

2. Combine the brownie mix, next 3 ingredients, and ¼ cup water, and bake according to package directions. Pour the batter into 1 prepared pan. Bake at 325°F for 30 minutes or until a wooden pick inserted in center comes out clean.

3. Meanwhile, place the butter in a large microwave-safe bowl. Cover and microwave at HIGH 30 seconds or until melted. Stir in the marshmallows and marshmallow crème. Microwave 1 to 2 more minutes or until melted and smooth, stirring at 30-second intervals. Add the rice cereal, and quickly stir with a rubber spatula coated with cooking spray until cereal is coated.

4. Spoon the cereal mixture into remaining prepared pan; press firmly into pan with fingers coated with cooking spray. Cool until brownies are done.

5. Remove the cereal mixture from pan, retaining foil. Invert the cereal mixture and foil onto hot brownies in pan. Firmly press bottom of 1 (9-inch) square pan on top of foil for cereal layer to adhere to brownie layer. Cool completely (about 2 hours). Remove the brownies from pan; discard foil. Cut into 30 small rectangles.

6. Place the bittersweet chocolate and white chocolate in 2 separate microwave-safe bowls. Microwave each at HIGH 45 seconds or until melted and smooth, stirring at 15-second intervals. Drizzle desired amounts of the melted chocolates over each rectangle; immediately sprinkle with the crushed espresso beans. Chill 10 minutes or until chocolate is set.

NOTE: We tested with Ghirardelli Chocolate Supreme Brownie Mix and Cocoa Krispies.

CHOCOLATE-ALMOND-COCONUT BITES

This is a very decadent take on mini chess pie bites. Adding the tropical flavors of coconut and almond to the mix makes them extra special.

MAKES 4 dozen • **HANDS-ON:** 25 minutes • **TOTAL:** 1 hour, 53 minutes

Vegetable cooking spray
½ cup sweetened flaked coconut
8 ounces (1 cup) unsalted butter, softened
1 (8-ounce) package cream cheese, softened
2 cups (9 ounces) all-purpose flour

½ cup (1¾ ounces) almond meal
2 large eggs, lightly beaten
1½ cups firmly packed brown sugar
2 tablespoons butter, melted
2 teaspoons vanilla extract
⅛ teaspoon table salt

½ cup chopped almonds, toasted
½ cup semisweet chocolate mini-morsels
Maldon sea salt (optional)

1. Preheat the oven to 350°F. Lightly grease 48 nonstick miniature muffin cups with cooking spray. Place the coconut in a single layer in a shallow pan. Bake for 5 to 6 minutes or until toasted, stirring occasionally. Cool completely.

2. Place the butter and cream cheese in a bowl. Beat at medium speed with an electric mixer until creamy. Reduce speed to low; gradually add the flour and almond meal. Beat just until blended.

3. Shape dough into 48 balls. Place balls on a baking sheet; cover and chill 30 minutes.

4. Preheat the oven to 350°F. Place 1 dough ball in each cup; press dough into bottom and up sides of cups, shaping each into a shell.

5. Whisk together the eggs and next 4 ingredients in a medium bowl. Stir in the almonds, mini-morsels, and toasted coconut. Spoon filling evenly into the pastry shells.

6. Bake at 350°F for 18 to 20 minutes or until filling is set. Lightly sprinkle tops of the tarts with sea salt while still hot, if desired. Cool in pans on wire racks 10 minutes. Carefully transfer the tarts from muffin cups to wire racks. Cool completely (about 20 minutes). Store in an airtight container at room temperature up to 1 week.

Crispy Espresso Brownie Delights

Chocolate-Almond-Coconut Bites

METRIC EQUIVALENTS

The recipes that appear in this cookbook use the standard United States method for measuring liquid and dry or solid ingredients (teaspoons, tablespoons, and cups). The information in the following charts is provided to help cooks outside the U.S. successfully use these recipes. All equivalents are approximate.

Metric Equivalents for Different Types of Ingredients

A standard cup measure of a dry or solid ingredient will vary in weight depending on the type of ingredient. A standard cup of liquid is the same volume for any type of liquid. Use the following chart when converting standard cup measures to grams (weight) or milliliters (volume).

Standard Cup	Fine Powder (ex. flour)	Grain (ex. rice)	Granular (ex. sugar)	Liquid Solids (ex. butter)	Liquid (ex. milk)
1	140 g	150 g	190 g	200 g	240 ml
¾	105 g	113 g	143 g	150 g	180 ml
⅔	93 g	100 g	125 g	133 g	160 ml
½	70 g	75 g	95 g	100 g	120 ml
⅓	47 g	50 g	63 g	67 g	80 ml
¼	35 g	38 g	48 g	50 g	60 ml
⅛	18 g	19 g	24 g	25 g	30 ml

Useful Equivalents for Liquid Ingredients by Volume

¼ tsp					=	1 ml
½ tsp					=	2 ml
1 tsp					=	5 ml
3 tsp	1 Tbsp			= ½ fl oz	=	15 ml
	2 Tbsp	=	⅛ cup	= 1 fl oz	=	30 ml
=	4 Tbsp	=	¼ cup	= 2 fl oz	=	60 ml
	5⅓ Tbsp	=	⅓ cup	= 3 fl oz	=	80 ml
	8 Tbsp	=	½ cup	= 4 fl oz	=	120 ml
	10⅔ Tbsp	=	⅔ cup	= 5 fl oz	=	160 ml
	12 Tbsp	=	¾ cup	= 6 fl oz	=	180 ml
	16 Tbsp	=	1 cup	= 8 fl oz	=	240 ml
	1 pt	=	2 cups	= 16 fl oz	=	480 ml
	1 qt	=	4 cups	= 32 fl oz	=	960 ml
				33 fl oz	=	1000 ml = 1 l

Useful Equivalents for Dry Ingredients by Weight

(To convert ounces to grams, multiply the number of ounces by 30.)

1 oz	=	1/16 lb	=	30 g
4 oz	=	¼ lb	=	120 g
8 oz	=	½ lb	=	240 g
12 oz	=	¾ lb	=	360 g
16 oz	=	1 lb	=	480 g

Useful Equivalents for Length

(To convert inches to centimeters, multiply the number of inches by 2.5.)

1 in				=	2.5 cm		
6 in	=	½ ft		=	15 cm		
12 in	=	1 ft		=	30 cm		
36 in	=	3 ft	=	1 yd	=	90 cm	
40 in				=	100 cm	=	1 m

Useful Equivalents for Cooking/Oven Temperatures

	Fahrenheit	Celsius	Gas Mark
Freeze water	32° F	0° C	
Room temperature	68° F	20° C	
Boil water	212° F	100° C	
Bake	325° F	160° C	3
	350° F	180° C	4
	375° F	190° C	5
	400° F	200° C	6
	425° F	220° C	7
	450° F	230° C	8
Broil			Grill

INDEX

Page numbers preceded by an F indicate the Flip Section.

ISBN-13: 978-0-8487-4964-4
ISBN-10: 0-8487-4964-2

Printed in the United States of America
First Printing 2016

Executive Director, Brand Development: Kristen Payne

Assistant Marketing Manager: Kathryn Lott

Creative Director: Chris Hoke

Marketing and Homes Fellow: Amy Gibbs

Manager, New Business Development: Laura Ferguson

Senior Editor: Katherine Cobbs

Editor: Meredith Butcher

Project Editor: Melissa Brown

Junior Designer: AnnaMaria Jacob

Recipe Developer: Pam Lolley

Food Stylist: Kellie Gerber Kelley

Photographers: Jean Allsop, Jessica Ashley, Iain Bagwell

Prop Stylists: Molly Clark, Kay Clarke, Lydia Pursell

Prop Coordinator: Jessica Baude

Assistant Production Director: Sue Chodakiewicz

Senior Production Manager: Greg A. Amason

Copy Editors: Donna Baldone, Adrienne Davis

Proofreaders: Rebecca Brennan, Polly Linthicum

Indexer: Mary Ann Laurens

Talent (Dog): Brady

Southern Living

YEAR-ROUND
Celebrations

Bonus Section

12 Special Occasion Menus & Decorating Ideas

FLIP THIS BOOK!

Nutty Chocolate-Coconut
Cake Bites

Tiny Caramel Tarts